PRAISE FOR *THE GOD-HUNGRY IMAGINATION*

The youth ministry world today is rethinking ma~·
paradigms, and practices, searching for dif
be more faithful and effective in contemr
offers a creative and important contribution
God-Hungry Imagination deserves to be widely

ᴄHRISTIAN SMITH
University of Notre Dame William R. Kenan Jr. Professor of Sociology
Director, National Study of Youth and Religion
Author, *Soul Searching: The Religious and Spiritual Lives of American Teenagers*

Sarah Arthur's *The God-Hungry Imagination* is welcome evidence that youth ministry has entered the postgadget era. She reminds us of a deep, if forgotten truth: human beings are storytelling, story-hearing, and story-living beings. She shows us how to cultivate youth's capacities for imaginatively dwelling in the Christian story. And, along the way, she blesses us with some very good stories of her own.

–FRED P. EDIE
Duke Divinity School
Assistant Professor for the Practice of Christian Education
Director, Duke Youth Academy for Christian Formation

Good stories, says Sarah Arthur, aren't out to make a point. They *are* the point. And they're powerful. Arthur even calls them subversive. They can wake you up and shake you up. When the Holy Spirit is present, they have the power to transform young lives and revitalize a tired youth ministry. Sarah seems to be onto something, and we who care about the spiritual health of young people would do well to carefully consider what she has to say.

–CHRIS LUTES
Editor, *Ignite Your Faith* (formerly *Campus Life*) magazine

Beyond propositions, beyond even the elements of theme and plot, lie mystery and meaning. Arthur takes us on a delightful journey down a path of imagination and narrative, inviting us to become "bards"—stewards of God's story to young people—and to have faith in the Holy Spirit's work in their lives. I'm looking forward to sharing this book with friends and colleagues.

–WILL PENNER
Youth pastor, speaker, author,
Editor, *The Journal of Student Ministries*

The God-Hungry Imagination challenges the "McJesus" culture of youth ministry that often seeks the latest fad to attract youth. A gifted storyteller, Sarah Arthur offers a thoughtful perspective on the use and power of story to transform thoughts and lives. With assurance and conviction, Sarah provides insight into imagination as a source of spiritual growth.

—**BETH MILLER**
Director of Youth Ministries, First United Methodist Church, Ann Arbor, MI
Founding director, The Strangely Warmed Players
Author of *Worship Feast Dramas* (Abingdon Press)

Having put together one too many supposedly "relevant" VBS or youth programs themed on a Cheez-Whiz Hollywood movie, I am hungry for this book. Sarah Arthur is a rare find. She is attentive to the needs of young people and eager to convey the richness of an orthodoxy that defies simple relevance. My eldest daughter, curious right now to answer whether *Star Trek's* cybernetic character Data has a soul, presses her church teachers to tell stories that intersect and complicate the popular stories to which youth are privy. Sarah Arthur will be a gift to those who help youth to know their own souls, and to know them saved in ways that invite us into a lifetime of story-searching and telling. —**AMY LAURA HALL**
Duke Divinity School
Assistant Professor of Theological Ethics
Director of the Doctor of Theology Program

Faith remains a vital part of most Americans' lives, but conveying that timeless message to new generations is a challenge, especially now that our culture is so fragmented and so many messages compete for our attention. In *The God-Hungry Imagination*, Sarah Arthur argues persuasively that pastors, teachers, and parents should reach back and reclaim the powerful narratives that were so important in reconnecting earlier generations with the faith. Standing in the tradition of J. R. R. Tolkien, C. S. Lewis, and Frederick Buechner, Arthur explains why it is so important to connect teenagers today with some of the timeless narratives handed down to us. It's in remembering those powerful stories that young people begin to connect the seemingly scattered elements in their own lives with a far larger, global community beyond the walls of their congregations. It's time to set aside any lingering anxiety that evangelical Christians may still harbor about our narrative imagination, she tells us, and trust in the faithful influences of stories that already have swept thousands of lives into the family of faith.

—**DAVID CRUMM**
Detroit Free Press Religion Writer

THE GOD-HUNGRY IMAGINATION

The Art of Storytelling
for Postmodern Youth Ministry

SARAH ARTHUR

WITH A FOREWORD BY
RON FOSTER AND KENDA CREASY DEAN

UPPER
ROOM BOOKS®
NASHVILLE

THE GOD-HUNGRY IMAGINATION
The Art of Storytelling for Postmodern Youth Ministry
Copyright © 2007 by Sarah Arthur
All rights reserved.

The Upper Room Web site: www.upperroom.org

UPPER ROOM®, UPPER ROOM BOOKS®, and design logos are trademarks owned by The Upper Room®, A Ministry of GBOD®, Nashville, Tennessee. All rights reserved.

Scripture quotations are from the New Revised Standard Version Bible, copyright 1989, Division of Christian Education of the National Council of the Churches of Christ in the United States of America. Used by permission. All rights reserved.

Poem "Royalty" reprinted from *Accompanied by Angels*, Wm. B. Eerdmans Publishing Company, 2006, copyright Luci Shaw. Used by permission of the author.

Poem "Tell Me a Story" copyright © 1985 by Robert Penn Warren. Reprinted by permission of William Morris Agency, LLC on behalf of the author.

At the time of publication, all Web sites referenced in this book were valid. However, due to the fluid nature of the Internet, some addresses may have changed, or the content may no longer be relevant.

Cover and interior design: Nancy Terzian/Nter Design, Nashville, Tennessee
Cover image (repeated on part pages): Kamil Vojnar/Photonica/Getty Images
Illustration on page 9: Sarah Arthur
First printing: 2007

Library of Congress Cataloging-in-Publication Data
Arthur, Sarah.
   The God-hungry imagination : the art of storytelling for postmodern youth ministry / Sarah Arthur.
      p. cm.
   Includes bibliographical references.
   ISBN-13: 978-0-8358-9919-2
   ISBN-10: 0-8358-9919-5
   1. Church work with youth. 2. Storytelling—Religious aspects—Christianity.
   3. Spiritual formation. 4. Imagination—Religious aspects—Christianity. I. Title.
   BV4447.A77 2007
   259'.23—dc22
                                          2007000449
Printed in the United States of America

To the Confirmands
of Petoskey United Methodist Church
1996–2002
Thank you for living the Story with me.

ACKNOWLEDGMENTS

Many thanks to the wise heads and kind hearts that listened thoughtfully, offered insight, read countless drafts, or in various other ways nurtured this book to fruition: Kenda Dean, Fred Edie, Ron Foster, Miranda Hassett (and Griffin!), T. J. Lang, Enuma Okoro, Robin Pippin, Joey Podhajsky, Leland Ryken, Kathleen Stephens, Anne Trudel, and Michael Ward. Also to Ellen Davis (with Dwayne Huebner), Richard Hays, and Wesley Kort of Duke University for suggesting resources and sparking my own creative imagination. Three cheers to the staff of the divinity school library for letting my "graduate spouse" ID card count for something more than admittance to women's basketball games (go Blue Devils!). Also to my coffee/lunch/e-mail buddies—Jami Blaauw-Hara, Sarah Kerr, Christy Polk, Tracy Tooley, and Claire Wimbush—for nurturing my spirit. But above all, to my husband, Tom, who never once suggested that a hungry imagination may be one thing, but a hungry tummy is quite another, and could I possibly consider a different career besides freelance writing, at least until we graduate from seminary?

CONTENTS

Tell me a story.

In this century, and moment, of mania,
Tell me a story.

Make it a story of great distances,
and starlight.

The name of the story will be Time,
But you must not pronounce its name.

Tell me a story of deep delight.

—Robert Penn Warren

FOREWORD

When my (Ron's) daughter Christine was four, she landed the leading role in our church preschool Christmas pageant. I'm happy to say that I didn't have to pull any pastoral strings to make this happen. Truth be told, she made a very good Mary, because she was quiet, serious, and earnest—all good qualities for portraying the mother of Jesus, I suppose. But what I remember most about the magical Advent and Christmas season that year was not the pageant itself. She did fine in her blue head covering and acted appropriately reverent and maternal, holding the plastic baby Jesus as she stood next to a somewhat distracted Joseph. The pageant itself was a hit, videographed and photographed by all the parents who attended.

No, what I remember most was driving around our community all that December with Christine. Anytime we saw a nativity scene on someone's lawn, she piped up matter-of-factly from the back-seat, "There I am." You see, she wasn't just playing a part. She had become part of the story. She was Mary in the Christmas story.

Theologian Stephen Crites says sacred stories are like dwelling places—like booths or tabernacles. We don't tell these stories as much as we inhabit them. Every Advent and Christmas season, I pray to experience the wonder and deep involvement of my then four-year-old daughter. I pray that personal engagement will trump professional detachment—that I will be able to step out of my role as a pastor, as the storyteller, and into the story itself. Like young Christine, I yearn for the capacity to fully exercise my God-hungry imagination, to borrow Sarah Arthur's image. Those of us in ministry probably feel this deep longing for everyone we serve and care for: that we'll find a way to engage people in God's story so they will claim their place in it.

Instinctively and empirically we know that stories have the power and the potential to capture hearts and imaginations—we're just not sure how or why this is so. We have seen it happen again and again: on the mission trip, when a seventeen-year-old's faith finally comes together as he helps right the trailer Hurricane Katrina washed off its foundation; in the funeral service, when the friends of the teenage girl killed in a car accident discover themselves bound to her in the story of Christian hope; in Communion, when young people enact a simple drama that somehow invites Christ to show up in the world again and again through bread and cup—and he does.

What surprised us when we read Sarah Arthur's *The God-Hungry Imagination* was how much it moved us—intellectually, pastorally, and spiritually. In this gem of a book, she offers the church neither a recipe (think: "how to tell good stories" in the service of ministry) nor a clinical dissection of the inner workings of narrative and imagination (though her analysis is keen and her insights exhibit profound understanding in this regard). This book contains plenty of substance—but also a surprising splash of theological artistry. Sarah Arthur creatively draws us into the rhythms and interconnections between heart, mind, soul, spirit, and story so that we may experience texts in a firsthand sort of way. The core of her message is that effective ministry to and with youth isn't simply enhanced by theological imagination. Ministry with young people—in fact, ministry with anybody—intrinsically relies on imagination to vividly and compellingly invite others into God's presence. Put another way, precepts and principles have their place, but God seems to prefer stories, calling on people with consecrated imaginations to mediate the ongoing drama of salvation in Jesus Christ.

She does all of this gracefully through winsome and colorful prose that doesn't just dissect the theological imagination; her writing itself incarnates and demonstrates theological imagination at its best. This is not a book that will simply inform you. Sarah Arthur's intent is to transform your soul and ministry, to help you reenvision your life in the light of the gospel itself. We predict that when you get to the end, you will be at a different place than you are right now, reading this preface. Like a good sermon, *The God-Hungry Imagination* carries you along until you suddenly realize that, at some point along the way, you have been swept up into a larger Story—*the* Story—and into God's waiting arms.

—RON FOSTER AND KENDA CREASY DEAN
Authors of *The Godbearing Life*
Epiphany 2007

PREFACE

I n 1998, when I was already burned-out from three difficult years in full-time youth ministry, I stumbled upon a resource that became a lit match on my dry brush pile of discouragement. The book was *The Godbearing Life: The Art of Soul Tending for Youth Ministry*, by Kenda Creasy Dean and Ron Foster.[1] I gathered a handful of other area youth workers; we read through the book over the course of several months, discussed the questions, and encouraged one another in what often feels like the most bewildering and con-flicted ministry of the church. Among other things, Kenda and Ron challenged us to put people over programs and to nurture our own spiritual health along the way. And we listened.

But the book also touched upon a concern that was already growing in my mind and has grown ever since: *how the church imparts biblical and theological content to its young people.* As Kenda and Ron put it, "Believing in God is not the issue; believing God *matters* is the issue."[2] How are the church's core theological beliefs expressed to, embraced by, and articulated by the next generation? In what sense do today's youth feel part of an ongoing story that matters—not only for the present but for eternity?

In 2002 I took a leap of faith away from full-time church ministry. I was tired of all the things that make youth workers tired. But I was even more tired of living a strange duality for so many years:

I loved kids—loved nothing more than to see them get excited about the adventure of faith—but I preferred books to people, generally speaking. I'm not proud of this preference; it's the dark side of the contemplative life. Books are much more manageable than teenagers. They don't forget their permission slips. They don't disappear right when you think things are going well. They don't cry in your office, yell at you in the parking lot, or talk about you behind your back. But more importantly, books will sit quietly on a shelf if you decide you've had enough of them for the time being. Monks have known this secret for centuries.

So all along, literature had been my first impulse, but youth ministry had been my calling, and my biggest conundrum was how to blend a love of story with a vocation that required organizing paintball events for vanloads of twelve-year-old boys. Reading Dostoevsky's *The Brothers Karamazov* didn't seem like exactly the best way to prepare for junior high youth group on Sunday night. Or was it?

A few months after I finished my final week of full-time ministry, I ran into a former student in the movie theater lobby, coming out of *The Lord of the Rings: The Two Towers*. It was his third time seeing it, my second. I asked him what he thought about it, and he said, with a look of wonder and awe on his face, "It's the best movie I've ever seen." The only other time I'd seen him look like that was at confirmation camp in seventh grade, on the last night around the campfire, gazing up at the stars. Something had happened to him. Something big.

And that really struck me. My literary training had taught me that J. R. R. Tolkien, author of *The Lord of the Rings*, was a committed Christian—he had been, in fact, instrumental in the conversion of his friend and colleague C. S. Lewis from atheism to Christianity back in the 1930s. So I knew this was more than just an ordinary story we'd seen in film. The other idea that struck me was: here was a pop-culture phenomenon ripe with teachable moments, with an audience of thousands (millions?) like this kid, totally soaking it up, a ministry opportunity just waiting to happen.

Suddenly my literary background—the part of me that loves stories—collided with my youth-ministry background. It was as if you could hear a "clang" as the two pieces finally fit together. It all seems like a big "duh!" to me now, but back then it was like a lightning bolt. Story is the primary way we impart what really matters to the next generation. Stories have the potential to embody biblical and theological content in ways that sink into the imagination, take root, and grow. And stories are how I myself was formed spiritually as an adolescent in a Christian community that lacked much in the way of youth programming. If it happened for me, why not for others?

It's taken me a few years to get a handle on what all this means for the big picture—the implications not just for me personally but for the church as it attempts to share the gospel within a postmodern context. Not long after that encounter in the theater lobby, I dived into the adventure of writing for youth about spiritual themes in classic literature and film. Since then, my concern about meaningful biblical and theological content has continued to grow; so a few years ago I began toying with the idea of a follow-up to *The Godbearing Life*

> *Story is the primary way we impart what really matters to the next generation. Stories have the potential to embody biblical and theological content in ways that sink into the imagination, take root, and grow.*

that would focus on the story (not merely the message) we are passing on to the next generation, and how that story is heard, received, embraced, and lived. In short, while *The Godbearing Life* addressed the need for meaningful *community* (communion) in youth ministry, *The God-Hungry Imagination* would address the need for meaningful *content*.

I was well into the project, with the deadline approaching, when I finally picked up another book I'd been wanting to read since its release: Christian Smith and Melinda Lundquist Denton's landmark study *Soul Searching: The Religious and Spiritual Lives of*

American Teenagers.[3] The results of the National Study of Youth and Religion confirmed my personal experience in ministry as well as my ongoing thoughts about "pervasive teen inarticulacy," not only in how teens express their beliefs but "how those beliefs connect to the rest of their lives."[4]

The God-Hungry Imagination is born out of my personal observations on how the church might effectively address these issues, combined with reflections on what theologians, artists, and educators have begun to understand about the relationship between imagination, story, and spiritual formation.

This book is intended for youth pastors and leaders who work with postmodern youth, for readers who have used *The Godbearing Life* as a youth ministry resource and are looking for other books in that vein, and for postmoderns themselves (of which I am one by accident of birth) as we try to express both the gospel to our peers and the struggles of postmodernism to our elders. You'll notice that the end of each chapter includes questions for reflection and discussion, as well as an "Idea for the Road" to consider for your own ministry setting. I hope you'll get the chance to process and pray about this material, as I did *The Godbearing Life*, with colleagues and friends facing similar issues. Whom could you invite to join you on this journey?

PART I

POSTMODERN MINISTRY

How do I happen to believe in God? . . . Writing
novels, I got into the habit of looking for plots.
After awhile, I began to suspect that my own
life had a plot. And after awhile more, I began
to suspect that life itself has a plot.

—FREDERICK BUECHNER

The seventh graders straggle into the darkened youth lounge in
their pajamas, toting pillows, Bibles, and flashlights, according
to instructions. The room is lit by a single candle. They plop onto
the couches, chattering, giggling, thwacking each other with pillows. Then gradually they grow quiet. Candlelight flickers on the
walls, casting shadows on their faces. Nighttime silence settles
around the room, a hushing spell on the spirit. The students hold
their breath. Something is about to happen.

Their youth leader opens a book.

"It was a dull autumn day," she reads aloud, "and Jill Pole was crying behind the gym."

For the next twenty minutes she reads the first few chapters of what most people consider a children's book: *The Silver Chair*, by C. S. Lewis. She takes it at a leisurely pace, pausing at just the right moments, altering her voice to represent different characters, building the tone and pace at the exciting parts. When Eustace falls over the cliff in the strange land on the other side of the door in the wall, a tense silence fills the room. Each young person has forgotten the others. Like Jill, they are there at the cliff's edge, feeling the updraft, battling nausea. They can hear the wind, smell the grass, taste the salt tears as she sobs in fear. They, too, grow thirsty after a while and shrink from the great beast, the Lion, who waits at the edge of the stream. They wonder how the Lion can speak, and how he seems to know all about Jill—how he knows that before their adventures, Jill and Eustace had been calling out for a mysterious Someone named Aslan.

"You would not have called to me," says the Lion, "unless I had been calling to you."

And the leader closes the book.

The listeners groan with disappointment, begging for more.

"Tomorrow," she promises, "we'll find out what happens. Right now, let's talk about the Lion."

CHAPTER 1

A "NARRATABLE WORLD"?

Why does anybody tell a story? It does indeed have something to do with faith, faith that the universe has meaning, that our little human lives are not irrelevant, that what we choose or say or do matters, matters cosmically.

—MADELEINE L'ENGLE

It's one of my favorite memories from my years as a full-time youth director: eleven seventh-grade confirmands, ramped up on sugar and the excitement of their first overnight retreat together, suddenly swept into the magic of a fantasy story written by a Christian storyteller who knew exactly what he was doing. In his essay "Sometimes Fairy Stories May Say Best What's to Be Said," C. S. Lewis famously asked why it was always so hard to "feel as one was told one ought to feel" about the story of the Christian faith, including the Passion of Jesus. He wrote:

> Supposing that by casting all these things into an imaginary world, stripping them of their stained-glass and Sunday school associations, one could make them for the first time appear in their real potency? Could one not thus steal past those watchful dragons?[1]

As youth workers, we know exactly what Lewis means by "those watchful dragons." In our materialistic age, young people are bombarded on all sides by voices claiming to have something they need. Sophisticated consumers, they're naturally resistant to anything that appears to be manipulating them into certain behaviors or beliefs—Christianity included. Thus many of them have posted the dragons of cynicism and skepticism at the gates of their souls, and it's these beasts we youth workers are up against when it comes to imparting biblical and theological content to this generation. Somehow we, like Lewis, must "steal past those watchful dragons" in articulating the gospel and imparting the theological language of faith. That is the task I wish to explore in this book.

[RE]DEFINING POSTMODERNISM

Cultural theorists tell us that cynicism and skepticism are to be expected because, after all, we've entered a "new" era called postmodernism. No doubt you've read enough about it to write your own version of what follows, but here's a quick summary. Postmodernism, according to such theories, follows the Modern Enlightenment Project of the eighteenth and nineteenth centuries, in which humankind was eternally optimistic about its evolutionary progress toward the ultimate good. Moderns believed every problem had a solution; human reason and scientific certainties had finally overcome the Dark Ages, or would eventually. And yet when "enlightenment" also produced the atomic bomb and the Holocaust, modern idealism quickly began to erode in the popular imagination, even as it had already begun to erode within the worlds of philosophy and art.

Thus many cultural commentators believe we are now thoroughly in the grip of a new era, a time when people are suspicious of the "myth of progress" and hence of any attempt to make some kind of narrative sense of the past, present, or future. The "information age"—or shall we say the "entertainment age"—has certainly changed the way communication is processed. We live in a generation that values images over words. (If you're unsure about this, pick up the latest issue of *Relevant* magazine, marketed to young Christians and seekers.) Such realities are generally chalked up to postmodernism, though it's important to mention that other commentators believe we're merely on a train pulling out of the station of modernism, but we haven't yet arrived at whatever's next. Writes Robert Jenson, "While the Western world is now 'post'-modern in the sense that modernity is dying around us, it is not 'post'-modern in the sense that any new thing is yet replacing it."[2] However, for the purposes of this book I will refer to this transition as postmodernism, since there aren't many other alternatives at the moment.

From within the church, most everything we're hearing about postmodernism says that propositional truth claims and rational argument are poor starting points for communicating Christian faith to this generation. I'm personally skeptical that *anyone* in the history of Christendom has been effectively argued into the kingdom without a lot of other factors at play—and, incidentally, it's those other factors I'm primarily interested in. But even so, undeniably the American church is up against something it hasn't often faced in its history: the astounding illiteracy and inarticulacy of the mainstream populace regarding theological and biblical concepts. Ask any middle schooler in your youth group what the word *idol* means, and she or he will probably say, "It's, like, someone you look up to who sings really good." Meanwhile, relativism and pluralism now infuse so much of popular culture that our young take it all for granted. As postmodernism completes its cultural coup, alarm bells are ringing in the church steeples, calling us to mobilize and . . . do *what*, exactly?

> *The American church is up against something it hasn't often faced in its history: the astounding illiteracy and inarticulacy of the mainstream populace regarding theological and biblical concepts.*

It's in this context that we find ourselves called to minister, and many of us spend our days carefully trying to discern how much of the postmodern ethos presents new opportunities and how much of it presents a threat to the gospel, all the while navigating the bewildering mess in between. The following example is not unusual.

A few years ago my husband, Tom, led an adult Sunday school class using the book *Four Views on Salvation in a Pluralistic World*.[3] The old liberals in the class (moderns at heart) asked, "What if there's more than one path up the same mountain?" This was what they were expected to ask, in their lovable benignity; and once upon a time they sounded pretty radical. But then a young woman, the only other twenty-something in the room besides Tom, blew them all away by suggesting, in essence, "What if there's more than one mountain?"

> *We can no longer assume that when we say a word like grace, our young people have even the faintest grasp of what we mean.*

Liberals and conservatives alike are floundering. All the old arguments have lost their power. But I suspect that it's not propositional truth claims or rational debates that are the problem per se, but the vagueness of the language we use to articulate theological ideas. We can no longer assume that when we say a word like *grace*, our young people have even the faintest grasp of what we mean, much less any interest in our three-point sermons about it. Something more fundamental is at stake: something that gets at the heart of language itself and how the human mind comprehends and articulates what it takes in from the outside world.

So we've come down to it. Since all other on-ramps to the communication highway appear closed, story has become the new buzzword in "emergent" ministry conversations. And while this may cause panic among rhetorical types who don't feel settled till they've taught somebody The Four Spiritual Laws, others think there just might be something to this whole narrative idea. As a longtime student of literature, I feel like a librarian who suddenly finds the aisles overrun by wide-eyed tourists toting guitars and basketballs. But as a youth worker, I also recognize many of my colleagues in the crowd.

Everyone's talking about metaphor and the nature of narrative, as if these are new discoveries rather than the very building blocks of language and understanding (not to mention faith). But few seem able to articulate just exactly what we mean by *story*, or why it works, or why it's so important in postmodern ministry—or even what we're supposed to do with it beyond the occasional sermon illustration or movie clip. Is it merely about adding a bunch of bells, whistles, and sensory experiences to worship and teaching, or is there more going on here?

POSTMODERN MINISTRY: TWO STRUGGLES

I believe there's more going on, and the evidence is nothing less than the slow exodus of youth and their families from Sunday morning worship over the past few decades, no matter what new bells and whistles the church employs. This is not about finding a new ministry trend or method that will fix the problem. It's about a profound reorientation of the way American Christians approach both corporate ministry and personal faith. In particular, we face two key struggles:

STRUGGLE 1: *Loss of the communal story or "metanarrative."* Pluralism and relativism aside, the church's primary angst is due to the loss of the Master Narrative (known as *metanarrative*, or overarching story) that defines the church and thus the individual Christian. Historically we've believed that our world's story is one that the God of scripture is telling, with a coherent beginning, middle, and end. This story has shaped Western culture for most of its existence. But despite the fact that Christianity could be considered "one of the oldest continuing metanarratives still in business,"[4] we can no longer assume that postmoderns in the pews believe they inhabit a "narratable world."[5] It was modernity, says Robert Jenson, that first dismantled the Narrator and attempted "to live in a universal story without a universal storyteller." But when the storyteller was lost, the story itself was lost. And when the story was lost, so were the people who once held it. Postmoderns have inherited the wind.

With the loss of story comes the loss of language for talking about the story. Overwhelmingly, according to *Soul Searching*, today's youth are "*incredibly inarticulate* about their faith, their religious beliefs and practices, and its meaning or place in their lives."[6] And, we can safely add, so are their parents. This isn't merely a question of what's getting lost in translation; it's a question of whether or not translation is happening at all. When the stories are lost, the language goes too.

> *When the story and language are lost, the community's unique identity fades away.*

Meanwhile, the prevailing attitude of "chronological snobbery" (the tendency to cut ourselves off from the past, including the stories that once defined us)[7] leads to the gradual loss of group memory, identity, and the sense of interconnectedness with other Christians across time and distance. When the story and language are lost, the community's unique identity fades away.

From what I've seen, these issues affect conservative and liberal churches of all stripes and how they tell the story of faith to the next generation, particularly in worship and discipleship, and how those generations respond. Not surprisingly, youth ministers find themselves on the front lines when it comes to encountering this aspect of postmodern shift, the loss of our communal story. (So *that's* why we're so tired!)

STRUGGLE 2: *A failure of the imagination.* Recently I asked a class of confirmands to write an answer to the question, "Why is faith important?" Their answers ranged from highly articulate about what God in Christ has done for us, to nothing—a blank space at the bottom of the page. The in-between answers fascinated me most. Here's one: "[Faith is important] because without faith you wouldn't be that confident or strong mentally. It helps you through the day, having faith in something."

Having faith in something. I can't think of anything farther from historical, biblical Christianity than that—except perhaps having faith in nothing. But this student isn't an isolated case. In *Soul Searching* the authors famously identify the current "religion" of American youth to be "Moralistic Therapeutic Deism"—even when those youth claim to be Christians.[8] In a nutshell, the three main values of this belief system are (1) religion helps you be a better person; (2) religion helps you feel good about yourself; and (3) God is there to help you when you need it but otherwise makes no claims on your life, time, or resources. "Spirituality is thus renarrated for all comers as personal integration, subjective feeling, and self-improvement toward individual health and personal well-being—and no longer has anything to do with, for example, religious faith and self-discipline toward holiness or obedience."[9]

In my estimation, Moralistic Therapeutic Deism points to *a colossal failure of the imagination regarding both the claims and demands of the gospel.* The failure isn't primarily on the part of youth or even their parents: it's on the part of the church. To use an example I'll refer to again, I recently got to know a youth director who serves in a mainline church that hasn't held a Good Friday service in years because it's "too depressing." This church skips right to Easter. Needless to say, my friend finds this bypassing of Good Friday distressing, particularly as she interacts with an entire generation that has never heard the Crucifixion narratives. Out of desperation one year she held a youth lock-in on Good Friday and showed *The Passion of the Christ*—a controversial decision that also happened to change a few kids' lives.

And yet her church isn't an anomaly. Nor are the mainline denominations the only culprits. At the other end of the spectrum, I recently visited a seeker-driven, nondenominational church that had all the technological bells and whistles, complete with a hip young preacher on stage in jeans and a T-shirt; but I heard the name of Jesus mentioned only *once* the entire time, tucked away in the last line of a contemporary praise chorus. There was no reading of a Gospel lesson, no sacrament of Communion, no call to serve or even join a small group, no cross to be found anywhere in the sanctuary. Everything was geared toward making me, the "seeker," feel happy and entertained without any strings attached.

If these churches serve as any indication, *Soul Searching* is dead-on accurate about the current spiritual climate in America. Rarely are youth challenged to take up their cross and follow Jesus down the narrow road called faith—but even when they are, they can't imagine what that really means unless someone famous makes a movie out of it.

Rarely are youth challenged to take up their cross and follow Jesus down the narrow road called faith.

Without story to engage the imagination, there's no sense of a narratable structure (beginning, middle, end) that connects a young person to the wider world. Without past or future, it's difficult to find meaning in the present. Hence the youthful complaint that church isn't personally relevant, which is a polite way of saying it's absurd. Well, duh. In a world where the immediate impulse of the present is king, very little that deals in eternals seems relevant. But there's also the issue of comprehension. We mustn't forget that the original meaning of the word *absurd* was deaf or muffled. So the problem could be with the hearer or with the transmission, or both. Today's youth have not developed the "ears to hear" what the church is saying; on top of that, the church tends to mumble when it speaks to teens. How do we address these issues?

Meanwhile, story hasn't completely disappeared. Even though universal metanarratives are largely absent, personal "I" narratives are everywhere. The popular imagination is saturated with self-obsessive stories in film, television, advertising, music, MySpace, and YouTube—but this is the equivalent of bingeing on junk food while dying for want of substance. The postmodern imagination is starving for some kind of narrative bigger than itself—hence the seemingly counterintuitive and almost cultlike followings of such mythic stories as *The Matrix* and *The Lord of the Rings*. As with every generation preceding them, postmoderns are hungry for lasting significance, starving for transcendence. Their imaginations crave the things of God. But too often they're unable to recognize sustenance when it's offered by the church, or the church itself offers the stone of "relevance" when its children ask for bread.

POSTMODERN MINISTRY: TWO RESPONSES

So what must be done? We turn to our resident thinkers, for starters. Scholars in such diverse areas as theology, developmental psychology, literary criticism, and education have begun to take narrative and the imagination more seriously in the last forty years or so (in literature much longer)—but for whatever reason, this trend hasn't trickled down to youth ministry. Only recently have pastors and Christian educators begun to reorient their thinking in light of these disciplines. So this book attempts to bring some of the ideas I've gleaned from these studies to bear on how we do youth ministry today, particularly in offering two responses to the two struggles discussed earlier.

RESPONSE 1: *Reclaiming the imagination's vital role in spiritual formation.* If part of what we're up against in postmodern ministry is a communal failure of the imagination regarding the claims and demands of the gospel, then we should take a serious look at this thing called the human imagination. What is it, anyway? What role does it play in spiritual formation? What's going on with our students when they're sitting in a darkened movie theater, watching the powers of light battle the powers of darkness in an imaginary world? How do we nurture the imaginations of youth so that they have the "ears to hear" and the vision to live by the real-life gospel of Jesus Christ? We'll discuss this in part 2.

RESPONSE 2: *Reclaiming the church as the living story.* Next we define story and identify why and how it works in imparting meaningful content through the language and culture of faith. In other words, what is story? How does it work? Why does it work? In what way is our Christian faith a story? What about the church? What implications does story have for what church is and how it does ministry? We'll tackle these questions in part 3.

And finally, we'll consider the art of storytelling itself. In what ways do we engage in storytelling through our worship and discipleship? How can we as pastors and youth workers—and as the church together—become even more effective storytellers? Parts 4 and 5 will explore these issues.

When it all comes down, the church is the living story we're inviting young people to participate in. Again, to quote Robert Jenson: "If the church does not find her hearers antecedently inhabiting a narratable world, then the church must herself *be* that world." How do we help today's youth develop a genuine sense of belonging to the "narratable world" the church has to offer in Christ?

What kind of story is your church telling?

IMPLICATIONS FOR YOUTH PASTORS AND WORKERS

So the questions are raised, the gauntlet thrown down. As youth workers, we're often the first-response team in addressing the above issues; and I believe the implications for how we do ministry start with how we perceive our primary role.

THE YOUTH PASTOR AS BARD

To the average (mainline) pew-sitter, as far as I can tell, youth pastors are considered moral educators whose primary medium is entertainment. We're supposed to impart the important stuff—a combination of "judge not" and the Ten Commandments—but in a way that turns youth on rather than off. And what about parable, subversion, serious teaching of the church's theological language, or, to keep it simple, *Jesus*? Right. Well, that might be pushing it. Otherwise, as one parent complained to me, the youth program is "too Christ-centered."

Okay, I suppose the pew-sitters can have it their way—that is, if they wish to train up more Moralistic Therapeutic Deists. All I know is that in a world threatened by the loss of story, the task of Christian discipleship—specifically, catechesis or baptismal training—becomes a matter of life and death. It means imparting the substance of faith—namely the story (Bible), language (theology), and culture (worshiping community)—to a disciple or learner who is spiritually starving. This substance is the content of spiritual formation. But it's also about the learner's willing reception of that content and his or her determination to practice and live by it. In other words, if my confirmands don't have a markedly different response to the question "Why is faith important?" by the time our process is finished, the church will have failed them.

So I suspect this means youth pastors are to be not merely lecturers seeking to inform or stand-up comedians seeking to entertain but storytellers seeking to enchant. Specifically, we must become bards: poets charged with the task of keeping and imparting the stories, language, values, and beliefs of a culture. We are *wordsmiths*, as the ancient meaning of poet implies: "speech-weavers"[10] who take the many texts of our hearers' lives and thread them through the warp and weft of the Christian narrative until patterned meaning emerges. As Native American storyteller Ray Buckley puts it, "The storyteller is a weaver of images."[11] We are bards who wield the power of word pictures—that is, metaphors—carefully and skillfully, knowing that metaphor is not merely superfluous embellishment to the actual "point" but carries the potential to "steal past those watchful dragons" of our hearers' usual defenses when other forms of discourse fail.

That's why, in addition to defining imagination and story, this book seeks to give readers those tools of the storytelling trade that

> *We must become bards: poets charged with the task of keeping and imparting the stories, language, values, and beliefs of a culture.*

we find in literature and the arts; and to explore how these tools might equip the church—and the youth we serve—for telling and living the gospel.[12]

RECOGNIZING OUR NATURAL BLINDERS

The irony of youth ministry today is that many of us who work with postmoderns are ourselves products of postmodernism: youth workers between the ages of twenty-two and thirty-five who were born and raised in a postmodern world. Thus we aren't talking about "them" but "us." We find ourselves wearing the lens of a postmodern worldview without necessarily realizing it, and likewise we find ourselves chafing at the modern methodologies of our elders without understanding why. True, postmodernism opens exciting new (old?) doors for the way the church does ministry. But it also poses some unique challenges.

First is the challenge to humbly recognize that all of us—moderns and postmoderns alike—wear natural blinders that bias us toward a particular worldview, and this bias can (often unintentionally) eclipse the authority of both scripture and the church for our lives and ministries. As Ellen Davis of Duke Divinity School gently reminds us, "It is sin, not historical distance, which keeps us from hearing the message of Scripture as 'relevant,' that is, life-giving."[13] We need to reclaim an attitude of humility and patience with one another across the generations of the church.

Second is to confess our attitude of "chronological snobbery" toward those who came before us, and then see what we can learn from them, rather than simply shrugging off their way of doing ministry. Both moderns and postmoderns must be willing to try old things in new ways and new things in old ways. This is especially true with stories and storytelling—which, as far as I can tell, are some of the oldest youth ministry methods around.

And finally we must recognize those areas of postmodernism that pose a direct threat to the gospel and against which we must take a strong offensive stance for the sake of our peers and the youth we minister to. Yes, we may be postmoderns by birth. But we are Christians first. That is our story.

KEEPING IN STEP WITH THE SPIRIT

We have the wonderful opportunity to respond meaningfully to the church's struggles within postmodernism. Hence a word of encouragement and caution before we get into the nuts and bolts of imagination, story, and storytelling.

We must seek God's power and guidance through prayer. Only the Holy Spirit can unstop ears and "steal past those watchful dragons." I can read aloud *The Silver Chair* till my students are numb—and explain its spiritual symbolisms and parallelisms till the kids are comatose—but only the Holy Spirit can stir spiritual longing, insight, or transformation in their lives. If we trust Jesus' own storytelling approach, we must trust the Spirit to work in and through story without the need to interpret every metaphor, every parable, every time.

We must trust the Spirit to work in and through story without the need to interpret every metaphor, every parable, every time.

But we must also be ready to help youth articulate and defend their faith when they're ready to move from narrative to theology. The abstract terms such as *grace* that Christians use to express faith *do* matter for a young person's spiritual formation. We'll explore these issues in the final sections on storytelling.

CLOSING THOUGHTS

When it comes to our role as bards—both as individuals in ministry and for the church as a whole—the question is not whether a particular story or metaphor will "work," but why it works. Often it has more to do with the hearers than with the story—and by that I don't mean whether the hearers "speak our language" or "get" the cultural references or have the right context for what's being said, but whether they've developed the imaginative capacity to engage with the story, no matter how strange or culturally removed it may seem. Yes, the techniques employed by the storyteller do matter. And yes, the story itself matters, and whether or not it's a story worth telling. But far more insidious is the obvious problem (obvious at least to me) that we are storytellers within a generation whose imaginations are so overstimulated and underdeveloped as to render all stories absurd.

Thus our first task is not to ensure that our stories and metaphors are relevant but to ensure that our hearers are indeed listening.

QUESTIONS AND EXERCISES

1. What "watchful dragons" keep the youth in your congregation from hearing and living the gospel? How might you "steal past" those dragons?

2. Where do you see evidence of "Moralistic Therapeutic Deism" in your church, if at all? How does that affect the church's youth ministry?

3. What strikes you about the concept of youth pastor as bard? What might that role mean in your context?

IDEA FOR THE ROAD

At your next youth gathering, tape long sheets of butcher paper horizontally on the wall and invite the students to create a time line of the world's story (as they would tell it), including where they personally fit in and how they think the story will end. Then discuss any of the following:

- Does the world have a story? How do you know?

- Does everyone agree on the story? Why or why not?

- As Christians, which story do we believe?

- Where do you enter the story?

- How do you explain your thoughts to someone who doesn't believe the world has a story?

FARE FOR THE IMAGINATION

Philosophers like Charles Taylor argue that inarticulacy undermines the possibilities of reality. So, for instance, religious faith, practice, and commitment can be no more than vaguely real when people cannot talk much about them. Articulacy fosters reality.

—CHRISTIAN SMITH[14]

PART 2

IMAGINATION

There are more things in heaven and earth, Horatio,
Than are dreamt of in your philosophy.
—*Hamlet*, act 1, scene 5

A few years ago I received an e-mail from a guy in Tokyo who had come across my Web site and was interested in my (then forthcoming) book *Walking with Frodo: A Devotional Journey through the Lord of the Rings*. He wrote, in broken English, "Reading LOTR[1] had some important part to my conversion to Christ when I was a teen." Intrigued, I asked him to explain further. Here is his reply, with some clarifications:

As a member of Generation X, born in 1965, I grew up in the middle of a counterculture in metropolitan Tokyo. This led me to Eastern thinking and the occult—e.g., Osho

Rajneesh, TM Meditation, tarot cards, Hinduism, Taoism, Tibetan Buddhism, and mystic Islam. All these teachings say "Good and evil are the same" and "God and the devil are two sides of the same coin."

In that very moment, I read LOTR . . . The reading convinced me of the absolute difference between God and the devil. I began to chant "A Elbereth Gilthoniel" . . . and to pray to the deity called "El" in LOTR.[2]

Soon afterward, I went to the Billy Graham Crusade in 1980 in Tokyo and "officially" encountered Christ.

However, I now feel that my initial conversion was already started through the experience of reading LOTR. Something similar . . . in George MacDonald's *Phantastes* led C. S. Lewis to his initial conversion to Christ as written in *Surprised by Joy*.

After the Crusade, I was introduced to a local Salvation Army church. Now I am an officer (pastor) of the Salvation Army, serving as a tutor at a college for officers' training.

Whoa. For youth workers who are generally in favor of telling kids the truth straight up, this sounds like a near miss. What if he'd gotten his hands on *His Dark Materials* by the decidedly anti-Christian Philip Pullman instead? Or what if Billy Graham hadn't come to Tokyo? The guy could still be praying to El Whoever and wandering in a spiritual fog.

But that's not what happened. Instead, a story opened the door to faith in the life of a teenager, and he isn't the only one.

In fact, as this fellow noted, it happened to C. S. Lewis.

At the beginning of the twentieth century, the staunchly atheistic teenager picked up a copy of the fantasy novel *Phantastes*, written by Victorian minister George MacDonald. Lewis later wrote, "What it actually did to me was to convert, even to baptise . . . my imagination."[3]

When, years after this experience, Lewis finally committed his life to Christ, it was because his friend and colleague J. R. R. Tolkien (among others) understood the power of the imagination and of story to draw a person into the proper worship of God.[4] The rest is history. The "reluctant convert" went on to become one of the most celebrated Christian authors of the twentieth century.

Three things strike me about the above examples. First, as a youth worker, I'm struck by the absence of traditional church youth programming playing any role whatsoever. Bummer. (If anything, as in the case of Lewis, the church was partly responsible for his initial tack in the opposite direction. Bummer again.) Second, as someone intrigued by the modern-postmodern shift from atheism to pluralism, I find it fascinating that in both cases, the Christian underpinnings of a fantasy story rang truer than the prevailing cultural milieu. And third, the human thread that seems to connect these two examples isn't the presence of fantasy literature, but rather whatever it is about human nature that makes such narratives—or any narrative—capable of effecting spiritual stirrings in the first place.

The more I look into this issue, the more I'm convinced that the imagination is this mysterious thread: specifically, the imagination "baptized" and "sanctified" by the Holy Spirit. And as I reflect on ten years in youth ministry, I'm more and more convinced the same is true whenever a young person begins to embrace this thing we call faith. While defenders of Christianity attempt to barge through the front door of reason by arguing "the case for Christ," the Holy Spirit has been slipping unnoticed through the back door of imagination and effecting spiritual change from the inside out. Such seems to be happening without our permission or even notice, and it's time we started paying attention.

You're probably wondering, *how does the imagination work in spiritual formation?* We'll get to that in a bit. First we need to understand what the imagination is.

CHAPTER 2

DEFINING IMAGINATION

Mr. Dursley . . . hurried to his car and set off for home, hoping he was imagining things, which he had never hoped before, because he didn't approve of imagination.

—*HARRY POTTER AND THE SORCERER'S STONE*

For the past few years I've been on a quest to find a good definition of the imagination. To begin with, the task is rendered difficult by the general suspicion on the part of many decent Muggles[1] that the imagination—loosely understood as the image-making faculty—is somehow evil or at least something we're supposed to grow out of. We hear of a child who is considered "imaginative" but rarely of an adult who is. Or if so, that person is considered rather loopy and possibly even dangerous, especially in committee meetings.

No doubt we have Freud and the moderns to thank for equating imagination with fantasy and illusion and making it all negative, particularly in their shaming of theologians who might otherwise have been the front-runners in helping us create a healthier understanding.[2] Even now there's a tenacious tendency among both liberals and conservatives to equate imagination with making stuff up. The fact that *imagination* rarely appears in theological or biblical scholarship without some adjective attached to it—such as *baptized, sanctified, prophetic, paradigmatic, theological, sacramental*, and, yes, even *homiletical*—demonstrates just how suspect the word has become when offered on its own terms.[3] (Of course, I couldn't go three words into the title of this book without calling the imagination "God-hungry"!)

But this is nothing new. Even going back as far as Saint Augustine and farther,[4] ordinary Christians of all stripes have been cautious and even antagonistic toward the strange power the imagination can wield over the human soul, especially when one considers that idolatry, biblically speaking, is the worship of images. The knee-jerk reaction on the part of many conservatives to anything "imaginary" is precisely due to this ongoing legacy—which is why I'm often asked by parents and pastors, "What do you think about Harry Potter?" I think they're trying to gauge how dangerous I am. The funny thing is, my teenage friends have no clue what prompts such a question in the first place.

In spite of this habitual distrust on the part of many grown Christians, after much study I've concluded that (1) the best definitions of imagination to be found anywhere come from thinking Christians; and (2) there appear to be as many definitions as there are thinking Christians. The trick is wading through the possibilities to see if any common themes emerge that might be helpful for how the church engages in spiritual formation with youth. And that's precisely our task in this chapter.

IMAGINATION AS "IMAGE MAKING"

We start with the basic definition, the one that appears in most dictionaries: imagination is the image-making faculty that allows us to see and experience things that aren't "immediately present to the senses." The engineer can picture a bridge before she draws it to scale; we visualize the scenes in a novel as we read. We dream in images; we have vivid memories, recollections so real it seems as if the events are happening all over again. My seventh graders were there at the cliff edge with Jill Pole, and it was just as real as the pizza they'd eaten for dinner. It was now part of their personal experience.

We might even say we think in images rather than words. For example, what comes to mind when you hear the word *adolescent*? A sentence about cognitive development, scrolling across your brain like a line of type? Or the mental picture of a scowling kid with multiple body piercings—a visual stereotype drawn from a combination of *Rolling Stone*, YouTube, and dark memories from your own high school days? Image making is an undeniable role of the brain; and this can be good or bad, depending on how you spin it.

So how do Christians spin it? At first glance it seems as if image making gets a bad rap whenever it appears in scripture. Pagans are the ones who worship false images in the form of idols (Jer. 50:38), engage in divination by dreams (Deut. 13:1-3), and generally exchange "the truth about God for a lie" (Rom. 1:25). In other words, they believe the stuff they make up. Boo to the human imagination.

But at second glance we see an older story, one that involves human beings created in the image of God (Gen. 1:26) and Jesus restoring that image when we distorted it—Christ himself being the very "image of the invisible God" (Col. 1:15). So from the beginning, image making appears to be a divine enterprise. And if we consider the various ways the imagination is engaged throughout scripture— through dreams, visions, metaphor, poetry, prophecy, parable (not to mention the very act of reading)—every page begins to light up with evidence of the imagination's role in divine-human doings. Add to that the stories of people whose lives were transformed by the Holy Spirit's use of something other than logical reasoning (the visions of Cornelius and Peter in Acts 10 come to mind), and one could make a very good case for the imagination as vital to both conversion and sanctification. As Ellen Davis says, the imagination is "the human faculty that has the greatest potential for connecting us with God"[5]—or as Garrett Green puts it, "Imagination is the anthropological point of contact for divine revelation."[6]

So, theologically speaking, image making is a function of both our original design as creatures and our redemption as new creations. We were formed in the image of God and are being transformed into the image of Christ. But until his kingdom comes, we must recognize that the image-making faculty can either lead us astray or bring us home, depending on whether or not we've surrendered it to the Holy Spirit at any given moment. We see in a mirror dimly. In the end it may be most helpful to say that, as with the rest of our human nature, the imagination is capable both of sin and of grace.

As important as this definition is, the imagination as mere "image making" seems inadequate to account for the uniqueness of imagination as a distinctly human faculty that carries the potential to reorient our world. After all, a cat will play with a milk-carton tab as if it's a tiny rodent, while a sleeping dog will twitch and whine as it dreams of . . . what? . . . chasing a squirrel? My guess is the cat isn't transformed by batting around a piece of plastic, but a teenager in Tokyo is different for having read *The Lord of the Rings*. Saying the imagination is merely that which allows us to visualize the invisible doesn't adequately account for all that's going on.

IMAGINATION AS "CREATIVITY"

Perhaps we can gain some insight from another popular definition: imagination as "artsy-fartsy" creativity. "He's so imaginative," parishioners say about the autistic boy who runs around the church in his *Star Trek* costume, drawing pictures of spaceships and taping extra buttons to the doorways. Creative ability is what people generally think of when they say a person is imaginative in the positive sense (as opposed to delusional). The imaginative young person is thought of as right-brained, inventive, nice but kind of flaky, and given to daydreaming or doodling. Most likely you can think of one such person in your church or home. Usually he or she is not considered very practical (e.g., "Can I really finish this essay during lunch hour, in time for my next class?") but occasionally demonstrates a kind of weird intuition that others may learn to appreciate in time—or at least, I hope that's what my editors think of me.

On a higher, holier level, many Christian thinkers have seen a direct link between the creative impulse and the stamp of our Creator upon us (the *imago Dei*). Writes J. R. R. Tolkien, "We make in our measure and in our derivative mode, because we are made: and not only made, but made in the image and likeness of a Maker."[7] Dorothy Sayers, another Christian writer of Tolkien and Lewis's vintage, echoes this sentiment in her book *The Mind of the Maker* (a standard textbook in Christian art and literature courses): "The characteristic common to God and man is apparently that: the desire and the ability to make up things."[8] In short, human creatures demonstrate the mark or image of their Creator specifically by their impulse toward creativity and invention (which, incidentally, means the autistic child is just as fully human as anyone else).

George MacDonald links this impulse directly to the primary role or purpose of imagination, which moves slightly beyond mere image making. He says, "The imagination is that faculty which gives form to thought."[9] To *give form* is to give something physical shape and substance, to draw its elements together into a coherent and visible whole. It's what God did at the moment of creation, when the word, which had been only a thought in the divine Mind, was spoken into the "formless void" (Gen. 1:2). And it's also what God did in the Incarnation, when the Word took on flesh (John 1:14). Though Jesus "was in the *form* of God," he took "the *form* of a slave, being born in human likeness" (Phil. 2:6-7, emphasis mine). The invisible became visible. That which seemed like formless nonsense suddenly took on shape and substance—took on meaning. We could say that both creation and incarnation are the divine imagination at full throttle, rendering meaning into the void by giving form and substance to divine thought and character.

It's not hard to see how the human imagination engages the world in much the same way. We "image forth" our ideas, giving them substance and structure through various creative mediums,

> *Though Jesus "was in the form of God," he took "the form of a slave, being born in human likeness." The invisible became visible.*

including language, art, and even scientific experiment. We incarnate thought into form so that others can see what we see. The autistic boy doesn't just imagine the spaceship; he draws it.

So there's artsy-fartsy creativity, such as sculpture and drama, but there's geeky creativity too. There's just as much imaginative ability involved in such technical vocations as, say, engineering and architecture as there is in writing a novel. All of us, in one way or another, are engaged in what Tolkien referred to as "Sub-creative Art"[10]: giving creative expression to our unique inner thoughts and impulses, or what is generally called "making stuff up from scratch."

But as human creators we're not simply inventing stuff out of the blue. Long before Tolkien, Sayers, and even MacDonald came along, the Romantic poet Samuel Taylor Coleridge, in protest against the Enlightenment's habitual dismissal of the imagination in favor of reason, referred to God's as the "primary imagination"—which created the world *ex nihilo*, out of the void and chaos—and to the human imagination as "secondary."[11] In other words, we can only riff on the themes we already find in the created world. We can only receive that which comes from outside ourselves and then keep fiddling around with it (e.g., the autistic child doesn't invent *Star Trek*; he simply plays around with someone else's idea). The human imagination has little to do with self-expression and everything to do with other-expression; so while our imagination is uniquely inventive out of all of God's creatures, it is never purely so.

To sum up: creativity—or, more properly stated, invention—is a major role of the imagination. But again, that alone seems to fall short in describing all the imagination is or does, particularly in its apparent ability to help us make a kind of intelligible and even theological "sense" of the world. Yes, we can perceive forms and patterns in the created world. And yes, we like to make forms and patterns ourselves. But why does this invest the universe with any kind of meaning?

IMAGINATION AS "THE MIND'S EYE"

I'll never forget the moment. It was the summer after my seventh-grade year, and my father, a pastor, was in charge of the junior high class for our church's vacation Bible school. Since there were only two students, it felt rather like a tutorial: the three of us sat at a table with our Bibles as my father read the Old Testament story about Joseph's brothers coming to Egypt. We were into the whole fiasco with Benjamin and the allegedly stolen cup (see Gen. 43–44), when suddenly, at the moment when Judah offers his life in exchange for Benjamin's, it was as if someone poked me hard in the ribs.

"Wait!" I gasped. The other two stared. "I know! I know what's going on!" I babbled. "This is about Judah, right? And isn't Jesus, like, descended from Judah? So Judah was the one who offered his own life in exchange for his brother's, just like Jesus did for us. Wow! That's so cool!"

I remember the look of surprise and delight on my dad's face. It wasn't as though I'd been a stellar student of scripture up to that point, though I loved Bible stories. Something new was going on. My imagination had moved beyond mere daydreaming and image making to genuine intellectual engagement with the world of narrative. I was connecting the dots, putting things together in a way I hadn't done before. The experience was so powerful that I've never forgotten it.

This snapshot from my adolescence introduces an important point. The imagination is not somehow divorced from reason or the intellect: it's one of the primary ways we learn. I'm indebted to a literary colleague of mine for suggesting that in classical tradition, the imagination is considered "the mind's eye" (emphasis on *mind*), an actual faculty of the intellect. It's not the opposite of reason or logical analysis, as many people think, but is, rather, reason's intuitive sister. Yes, it includes the ability to "see" what isn't physically present, but this inner sight is *a way of knowing and understanding in its own right*. It arrives at knowledge by a different path than logical reasoning, but the result is still knowledge. So the novelist in your youth group is not less intelligent than the math whiz but intelligent in a different way.[12]

George MacDonald called imagination the "region of discovery."[13] It's the doorway to wonder, prompting questions that lead to such things as philosophy, scientific inquiry, and poetry. The unique path to knowledge taken by the imagination can be articulated as *the ability to both discover and create relationships linking otherwise unconnected experiences, images, or ideas.* It intuitively apprehends, synthesizes, and expresses connections between things. It isn't just making things up;

The unique path to knowledge taken by the imagination can be articulated as the ability to both discover and create relationships linking otherwise unconnected experiences, images, or ideas.

it's using the nearest natural, cultural, and linguistic tools to both apprehend and creatively express what it discovers. This is what was happening to me as I connected the dots between Judah and Jesus all those years ago.

It's worth noting that my random seventh-grade experience was not necessarily a conscious enterprise. One major difference between imagination and reason is that imagination often operates beneath the surface of analytical thought. Here I can't help thinking of Sherlock Holmes, musically brooding with his violin till the solution to the mystery presents itself. While reason is primarily a conscious enterprise that demands one to be aware of one's thought processes, imagination can be both subconscious (or preconscious, as with intuition) and it can be conscious and purposeful, as with creative or artistic invention. In any case, it is not, as many seem to think, irrational, though it does at times have a playful element that defies logical explanation.

"What do those squiggles in the sand mean?" asks the mother of her busy child at the beach.

"Um, I don't know," replies the child. He's making squiggles because he likes the pattern created by the dark, wet sand in the trenches and the light, dry sand on the ridges, and because he enjoys the way sand feels. So what is he learning about the sand as he plays? More than he can articulate right now.

"It looks like a fish," his mother says helpfully. "No," he replies, "it's a dragon." And before long he's begun connecting the squiggles, adding a claw here, a tail there, until his mother, satisfied, leaves him alone.

In partnership with playfulness, the imagination gives us the ability to find and make purposeful patterns and even plotlines: in other words, the ability to find and make meaning. Of Christ's commandment to love the Lord "with all your mind" (Mark 12:30), David F. White notes:

> The Greek word . . . for mind is not *nous* but *dianoia*, suggesting not abstract intellectualization, but instead includes the meaning, "Love God by the way you put things together." It has the meaning of coherence—how we make sense of our discrete experiences and endow [them with] meaning.[14]

We find a certain coherence or "rightness" in putting things together; our minds seek to bring order out of what feels like chaos or disconnectedness.[15]

So as a faculty of the intellect, the imagination is the mind's eye, the way we "put things together" and make sense of our world.

IMAGINATION AS "THE ORGAN OF MEANING"

Leave it to C. S. Lewis to say things clearly and succinctly. In his literary essay on metaphor "Bluspels and Flalansferes: A Semantic Nightmare," he writes: "For me, reason is the natural organ of truth; but imagination is the organ of meaning."[16] Typically, Lewis uses a metaphor to make a point about metaphor, to express why we think and speak in concrete expressions rather than in purely abstract statements (more on metaphors later). Our organs process elements so those elements can become useful to the body: for example, the digestive organs process food. So, according to Lewis, the "organ" of reason processes truth while the "organ" of imagination processes meaning. Reason chews on abstractions (e.g., the nature of justice) while imagination chews on narratives, images, and metaphors (e.g., the workers who came first are paid the same as those who came last).

From a spiritual standpoint, the application is intriguing. A young person can have at her fingertips all kinds of theological truths or facts, ideas or abstract statements—in short, the correct content of the faith—but unless that content is also identified with concrete images or experiences (even if at first those concrete images/experiences seem to have nothing to do with faith), abstractions will have little real meaning for her. The opposite is also true: experiences will remain amorphously disconnected from historic, biblical Christianity unless the truth is spoken to and grasped by her reason.

To put it bluntly, without imagination engaged in helping her process what a truth means, she doesn't yet fully embrace it. A powerful case for the importance of imagination in spiritual formation, to be sure! However, this doesn't therefore dismiss the critical role that reason plays in helping her find appropriate language to articulate and defend the meaningfulness of truth. Imagination is not superior to reason. Rather, it's *when reason and imagination finally catch up with each other that both the truth and the meaning of the gospel have the potential to "click" into an intelligible whole.*

My correspondent in Tokyo is a fitting example. Without *The Lord of the Rings*, it's doubtful Billy Graham's evangelistic message would have made much sense; and likewise without the message, it's doubtful my friend ever would have made the connection between Tolkien's fantasy world and the spiritual yet historic reality of biblical Christianity. C. S. Lewis's experience also fits this pattern.[17] "No man is saved by his imagination," quipped nineteenth-century Scottish preacher George Morrison. "It is a question if any man is saved without it."[18]

The human imagination hungers for substance, for meaning, for God. If it encounters a world without meaning, it slowly starves for lack of anything to chew on. The "organ of meaning" must have something to eat. Feeding the God-hungry imagination is, I believe, precisely the church's task in spiritual formation.

IMAGINATION AS "THE ABILITY TO SAY WHAT SOMETHING IS LIKE"

One more attempt at defining the imagination is worth noting; and will, I suspect, become more and more significant as this book progresses. It's what might be called *analogical ability*, or the ability to think in analogies—in metaphors.

Metaphor happens whenever something is described in terms of something else. For example: when ticked off, God is described as being "like a storm of hail" (Isa. 28:2). Let's break this down a bit. On the one hand, we have God, the divine personality, unseen and indescribable, a fuzzy image at best. On the other hand, we have dark clouds blasting chunks of ice from the sky, an unforgettable visceral experience that sends smart people scrambling for cover. And the analogy works. We grasp hold of it on a level deeper than logical analysis or abstract proposition. Thus, says Garrett Green, "Imagination is the ability to say what something is *like*."[19]

It starts with language itself. Metaphor theory explores the idea that all language is, in fact, metaphoric.[20] "We can explain nothing in terms of itself, but only in terms of other things."[21] For example, think of the word *remember*. Its root is *member*—as in the different parts or members of the body. So to *re*-member is to put the body back together again. When you close your eyes and picture your high school English teacher, you're putting together the different aspects of his or her physical characteristics, personality, voice, and various events. Like all the king's horses and all the king's men, you're attempting to put Humpty together again. You're re-membering that which has come apart due to time and distance. So the word *remember* is, in itself, a metaphor for the human experience of suddenly reconstructing, without necessarily even intending to, a body in one's inner mind.

Metaphor is also how children and nonnative speakers learn a language. The parent or host says, "Do you see that thing flying up there? It's called a plane. A plane is like a bird, except it's a really big machine that carries people inside—kind of like a car with wings." The imagination must be fully engaged to track that description. It must be able to picture a bird, a machine, a car, a wing, and somehow put them together into a composite image that makes sense. On top of that, it must be able to connect that image with the word *plane*.

There's something inherently mysterious about this process. One object (person, event, idea) is like something else while at the same time being its own self. We instinctively know when a metaphor doesn't work, but can we really put a finger on why? The best metaphors are a bit magical. They conjure connections that weren't there in our minds before, rather like the magician who pulls the quarter from behind someone's left ear. How did the coin—which has no business being anywhere except in the magician's pocket—end up there? We don't know, but the scenario worked. Somehow the imagination made the connection.

Needless to say, Christians swim in metaphor like fish in the sea. Spiritual formation requires some measure of analogical or imaginative ability, since we are, after all, dealing with an invisible God who can't be humanly grasped except in comparison to things that are, well, humanly grasped. Even God uses metaphors as self-descriptors, knowing that we require buffers between our small selves and God's own presence. The one exception is Jesus, who—we must never forget—is not a metaphor. Wrote the late theologian, Hans Frei, "The story of Jesus is about him—not about someone else, or about nobody in particular, or about all of us."[22] Jesus is himself, the image of the invisible God. Whoever has seen him, he says in John 14:9, has seen the Father. He's not merely an illustration or metaphor of God's mercy; he is God's mercy. This understanding of what is and is not metaphoric about our faith is an important theological concern worth discussing later in more depth.

In the meantime, we use metaphors to express the trinitarian relationship along with most other key theological concepts we embrace as Christians. "What is the kingdom of God like?" Jesus asks. "And to what should I compare it?" (Luke 13:18). Given how many of the parables, poems, and prophecies of scripture are built around metaphor, it soon becomes clear that we can't go more than a few chapters into the Word or a few steps into the faith without being asked to exercise the analogical ability of our imaginations—as I learned firsthand in seventh grade.

CLOSING THOUGHTS

In the end, a working definition of imagination is hard to pin down, but I'll give it a stab anyway. Taking into account everything we've discussed so far, we can say the imagination is the image-making faculty of the intellect that helps us discover, process, and creatively express coherent meaning. Or, to state it quite simply, imagination is how we put things together. It's how we make connections between thought and experience, word and image, self and other, seen and unseen. And its implications for spiritual formation are intriguing, to say the least, which is what we'll tackle in the next chapter.

QUESTIONS AND EXERCISES

1. How do your congregation's leaders generally perceive the imagination—as something good or bad? Why? How have you generally perceived it?

2. What strikes you about the concept of imagination as the "organ of meaning"? How might this concept inform your church's ministry to youth?

3. What role has analogical ability (the ability to think in metaphor) played in the spiritual formation of yourself and/or the students you work with? What significance might this have for worship and discipleship?

IDEA FOR THE ROAD

Using pictures from magazines or the Internet, have students create collages expressing what God is like. Then discuss: why did they choose those images and metaphors? How might they explain their collage to someone who isn't a Christian? With older students, ask how they might explain their collage to someone who disagrees with the images or metaphors they chose. In other words, are all metaphors created equal? Why or why not? At what point do we appeal to the biblical and theological metaphors of historic Christianity as the norm? And at what point do we craft new metaphors to speak to a new generation?

FARE FOR THE IMAGINATION

Science may pull the snowdrop to shreds, but cannot find out the idea of suffering hope and pale confident submission, for the sake of which that darling of the spring looks out of heaven, namely, God's heart, upon us his wiser and more sinful children; for if there be any truth in this region of things acknowledged at all, it will be at the same time acknowledged that that region belongs to the imagination.

—GEORGE MacDONALD[23]

CHAPTER 3

IMAGINATION AND SPIRITUAL FORMATION

Are we genuinely prepared to say that working in an office building or shopping in a mall is real, while reading Tolstoy is not? Which engages us most fully as thinking, feeling, believing, questioning creatures? Which best draws out our humanity? Which is most likely to change us? Which, then, is more real?

—DANIEL TAYLOR

One summer as I directed our youth confirmation camp,[1] two of my guys got hooked on the Redwall series by Brian Jacques. They spent every spare minute with their noses buried in those books, following the fate of the good creatures of Redwall Abbey in the battle against a fierce band of marauding rats. Sometimes it was all I could do to tear them away from the story and bring them back to the task at hand. And yet (to my adult volunteers' chagrin), I never told them to put the books away and be sociable in the van or otherwise. That's because, as both a Christian and a student of literature, I saw *Redwall* as more than mere entertainment; it was part of the camp curriculum. We were in the business of shaping their characters to become more like Christ, and if a story about little monastics squaring off with the forces of darkness didn't reinforce the point, what did?

But by Wednesday I was getting a bit annoyed, to be honest. There were only ten students altogether, so for one-fifth of my group to be checked out most of the time wasn't exactly helping us build community. But then came Wednesday night. That's when we surprised the students with a raid by the "secret police," who put us in lockdown for openly worshiping God. The students were challenged to try and escape into the woods to a secret meeting place for worship without getting caught and thrown in jail. We couldn't worship until everyone had arrived safely, so if someone got caught, the rest of the group had to tag them out of jail.

And so the game began. Off they ran, by twos and threes, into the darkening woods, with the secret police hot on their heels. The kids created diversions, staged jailbreaks, hid under logs, helped their friends, and eventually arrived—breathless and somewhat shaken—at the secret meeting place. There they learned about the early Christians, the persecuted church, the cost of discipleship, all the while glancing over their shoulders to make sure the coast was still clear. Finally, I asked if someone would close our meeting in prayer.

"I will," said one of my *Redwall* guys—who, I might add, was mostly unchurched because his dad was an agnostic. We all joined hands. "God," he said, "thank you for dying for us so we can be free and stuff. Please take care of the Christians in other countries who aren't allowed to worship you. Help us to not ever take faith for granted. Amen."

If I could've required every student to read *Redwall*, I would have!

THE TASK OF CHRISTIAN FORMATION

Nowadays the college department in which I received my undergraduate major is no longer called CE—Christian Education—but CF: Christian *Formation*. The change is born out of a growing awareness that *discipleship is primarily formative, not informative*: we are being formed into the image of Christ, not receiving a pile of information like a textbook. Formation is the content of faith. It encompasses more than just what happens in Sunday school or confirmation class but includes every aspect of the Christian life, from worship and service to the private spiritual disciplines of prayer and solitude. (And your church thinks you were hired just to run VBS!)

Yet too often in youth ministry we confuse *formation* with *formula.* We adopt a method of strategic programming designed by "experts" from afar and then try to conform youth to that particular developmental pattern. First we evangelize; then we disciple; then we send them out to serve, right? We try to fit our youth into this formula—x equals Kate or Chad—and then we create our programming accordingly. We're baffled when x doesn't respond or behave as planned. We're even more baffled when x goes off to Bible camp and comes back completely transformed by the influence of unknown integers who haven't been there for steps 1 and 2, as we have. Something far messier is going on with spiritual formation than mere formula.

> *Being formed in the image of Christ is the process and goal of spiritual formation; that's what we're working and praying toward; that's what we're helping youth to become.*

In spite of all this, the story of faith still has a narrative arc: a beginning, middle, and end. We do have a sense of where this whole thing is headed, even if we can't prescribe every stage of the journey for each unique individual. Being formed in the image of Christ is the process and goal of spiritual formation; that's what we're working and praying toward; that's what we're helping youth to become: "little Christs"—Christians who reflect the image of Jesus to the world. Writes Garrett Green,

> Being conformed to this image means shaping one's life after Christ's life, patterning one's own living according to the pattern of his story, following the example of Jesus.

> The *imago Dei* is thus restored not as some kind of spiritual substance ("soul") but in the "narrative shape" of the Christlike life.[2]

And this is precisely where the imagination comes into the picture, moved by the Spirit, tying together all those unknown integers that don't seem to fit the developmental formula until a meaningful pattern does indeed emerge.

Without the imagination, as we discussed in the previous chapter, youth are unable to see God's own image in themselves or others. They can't properly gauge how that image has been distorted by sin. They can't visualize the end result of their spiritual journey because they can't "see" Jesus, who is himself the goal. If they, like the interview subjects in *Soul Searching*, view God as "a combination [of] Divine Butler and Cosmic Therapist,"[3] then everything about them is oriented—or disoriented—around that distorted image. If a young person can't properly (i.e., theologically) visualize the Christ of scripture, or how his image connects to her everyday life, or what any of this has to do with the worshiping community, then all our programmatic efforts are vanity, a chasing after the wind.

But spiritual formation isn't merely about the end result; it's about the formative process itself. It's about the mysterious, artistic activity of the Spirit from the dawn of creation to the sunset each evening, in which previously unconnected elements are fashioned—formed—into a coherent whole. Remember how I said the imagination is what helps us put things together, which in turn helps us discover meaning? Consequently, a vital role of the imagination in spiritual formation is to help a young person make meaningful connections between the church, the world, and her life. Otherwise she remains in a swirl of chaos, a formless void, no matter how carefully programmed her church experience may be.

Imagination, through the creative activity of the Holy Spirit, can bring the separate elements of her world together. It's our job to be the cocreators.

THE ACTIVE IMAGINATION

Unfortunately, it's all too easy to point out examples in which an active imagination serves to thwart and distort the image of Christ rather than aid spiritual formation. We all know young people whose imaginations are powerful—possibly even hyperactive—except the outcome is disturbing. Pornography is one example. The shootings at Virginia Tech in the spring of 2007 are another. The postmodern phenomenon of virtual reality could be considered yet another—and, not incidentally, has close connections to the first two. All of these examples are marked by unhealthy use of the imagination centered upon the inability to make meaningful connections with real human beings and the real world. In these cases, "the sinful imagination, far from being a source of deliverance, becomes the most destructive weapon in the arsenal of human enmity toward God."[4]

Some might say the desire to escape is the problem. The postmodern world is by turns meaningless, scary, isolating, and mind-numbingly boring to the young. So they self-medicate by virtually exiting reality. The imagination becomes their portal to illusory worlds that bear little or no resemblance to the actual landscape of their daily lives. But, as Tolkien would say, the desire to escape is not the problem: "Why should a man be scorned if, finding himself in prison, he tries to get out and go home?"[5] To the God-hungry imagination, the fallen world is a crummy place much of the time; we rightly long for the land at the back of the wardrobe, the kingdom east of the sun and west of the moon. And yet despite the fact that many teenagers mistake Middle-earth for the true "home" Tolkien had in mind, we must not, as he says, confuse "the Escape of the Prisoner with the Flight of the Deserter."[6]

Here it seems important to draw a distinction between healthy and unhealthy escape. Unhealthy escape is when a teenager seeks to leave the "real world" and refuses to return; he loses sight of his true identity and cannot accept reality. Healthy escape, by contrast, is when a teenager retreats for a little while into another "world" that helps him see this one in a clearer, holier light. He willingly returns to waking reality with a better understanding of himself and his purpose for living. This, I believe, is what happened to my two *Redwall* guys at confirmation camp and to my friend in Tokyo. Writes Dorothy Sayers, "The child who dresses up as Napoleon, and goes about demanding the respect due to Napoleon, is not necessarily a little paranoiac with a Napoleon-fixation; he is just as likely to be an actor."[7] The same could be said for the young person who experiences something profound at Bible camp and comes home calling himself a Christian with more conviction than he did before. He's not necessarily a brainwashed Jesus freak with a Pharisee complex; he's just as likely to be a disciple.

> *The imagination has the potential to connect us with spiritual reality and even transform the way we view this physical world and operate in it.*

Clearly, an active imagination, when not transformed by the gospel and guided by the Holy Spirit, is just as prone to sin as any other aspect of our humanity. But it still has the potential to connect us with spiritual reality and even transform the way we view this physical world and operate in it. Thus someone such as Leland Ryken, professor of English at Wheaton College, Illinois, can consider the imagination a "means of grace"[8]; and, from a Wesleyan perspective, we can easily see how the imagination is one of the ways the Holy Spirit works *previeniently* in our lives—before we're even aware of God's presence. My friend in Tokyo is a great example: he can look back and see how God used a fantasy novel to till the soil of his imagination so the seeds of faith could be planted. Where would he be today if he hadn't read that book? And yet the same could be said of the Billy Graham event he attended. What strange, twisted ideas his active imagination might have produced without that evangelistic encounter!

So the crucial issue in spiritual formation isn't merely whether the imagination is active, but whether it's *healthy*.

THE HEALTHY IMAGINATION

So now we get down to the basic elements of what a healthy imagination looks like. We have plenty of examples of its opposite, but what are the defining characteristics of its vibrant and robust ideal? Taking all of our various definitions into account, it would seem that a healthy imagination is one that is nurtured in five key areas: (1) engagement, (2) meaningful synthesis, (3) vision, (4) empathy, and (5) creative response. We start with number 1.

1: *Engagement.* The healthy imagination, rather than drawing a young person into his own little world, connects him with a world larger than himself. Picture my two guys at confirmation camp, reading about an imaginary battle between good and evil (albeit, a battle between small rodents). Imagination is the "region of discovery" by which a teenager observes, takes notes, traces clues, follows ideas, and pursues the white rabbit of curiosity into an unknown universe not of his own making. He engages with that larger world through imagination; he takes in and receives what he finds there, making it part of his own experience.

2: *Meaningful synthesis.* The healthy imagination, fully operating as "the organ of meaning," helps a young person process the disconnected elements of both his inner and outer worlds so that coherent patterns emerge. Here we can't help thinking of Buechner's comment that as a novelist, he "got into the habit of looking for plots." A healthy imagination takes what it discovers and synthesizes it into something that makes sense, that carries meaning. Imagination begins to weave its own interior pattern.

3: *Vision.* Here the young person catches a glimpse of where that interior pattern might be headed, what sort of coherent image is emerging from the loom of her otherwise indecipherable and wacky life. Within the narrative arc of that pattern, she begins to sense what the next chapter might bring, what she herself can do about it. This may include vocational discernment, or it may even be insight into the transformative potential of the broader community in which she lives. It may even be a heartfelt prayer at the end of a crazy camp game. A healthy imagination shapes the young person's ability to hope.

4: *Empathy.* The imagination also allows a young person to experience the suffering of others by picturing what it would be like to be in their shoes. We could say he suddenly recognizes the image he sees in another human being. This gift of empathy is perhaps one of the most important factors in moral development, outstripping the threat of punishment as a healthy motivator toward right behavior. Peter Schakel writes, "Imagination is needed in the moral realm . . . to give meaning to morality, to connect its principles to life, to bridge the gap between theory and practice."[9] It gives the young person the ability to connect emotionally with a hurting world, just as my camper did in his closing prayer for the persecuted church. The imagination connects to emotion in such a way that elicits what follows: creative response.

5: *Creative response.* Here the imagination prompts the will to action. It may be through prayer, artistic expression, community service, prophetic preaching, or any number of outward responses; but whatever the case, the young person becomes a creator in her own right. She no longer merely imagines a world; she acts according to her unique abilities to help build and rebuild that world.

These are not the only areas in which the imagination is nurtured—we could add play, along with memory, and even analogical ability (which, as we said earlier, is the ability to think in metaphor)—but this list is sufficient to give us an idea of why a healthy imagination matters in spiritual formation. Put within the context of Christian scripture and tradition, we could say a healthy imagination enables a young person to (1) engage with divine revelation and the Master Story; (2) interpret a pattern within that story that both confronts and resonates with his personal experience (such as the traditional arc of creation, rebellion/exile, redemption, return); (3) claim a new vision for his role within the story as lived out in the community of faith; (4) empathize with human suffering through being able to see the image of Christ in others; and (5) respond creatively and faithfully out of that new understanding.

While the five functions adhere to a particular narrative structure, that structure is not meant to be formulaic or prescriptive. Spiritual formation will certainly not happen in exactly the same way for every young person and may be in fact more cyclical. For example, a teenager who finds himself empathetically engaged with a homeless person (as in #4) may find within that experience a sudden resonance with the gospel that he never had before (as in #2). The imagination helps to connect the dots, but the points may not follow a linear progression. Not every camper, for instance, had the same reaction to our secret service night as my *Redwall* guy. Some were just plain bored.

It's tempting to think that a truly healthy imagination, one that's firing on all cylinders, is possible only if we address the issue from the ground up, starting with the preschoolers in our congregations. Because (we wail), by the time they come to us, too much damage has been done; their imaginations have become too malnourished to be of much developmental use, right? But this is being overly optimistic on the one hand (what are the odds that all your current preschoolers will be on the roster for confirmation in eight years?) and overly pessimistic on the other. For the truth is, the students you have right now—the ones who sit in the pews, show up for Sunday school or youth group, and snooze through confirmation—are not beyond the reach of the Holy Spirit. If their imaginations are starved, you feed them; if they are thirsty, you give them something to drink. Trust the Spirit to bring the needed nourishment along the way.

> *It's tempting to think that a truly healthy imagination, one that's firing on all cylinders, is possible only if we address the issue from the ground up.*

NURTURING THE IMAGINATION

I hope it has become apparent by now that artists and other supposedly imaginative people don't have a corner on spiritual formation. Nor do children or even youth. All of us use our imaginations when it comes to faith, and all of us struggle to stay imaginatively healthy in this mostly neurotic, image-conscious culture. Writes Janine Langan, "We must tame and guard our own imagination if we wish to attend properly to reality. For the imagination always totters between that Wisdom, which played at the feet of the Creator before the stars sang together, and madness."[10] Nurturing the imagination becomes a vital task for each of us as individuals within the church, even as we seek to help youth make healthy, imaginative connections between the church, the world, and their lives.

It seems to me that the diagnosis of "pervasive teen inarticulacy" in matters of faith has to do with the inability to make those connections. A stroke victim struggles to articulate the image or concept she has in mind because the connection between the image and its corresponding word has been disrupted in the brain. It's as if the same thing has happened to our young people—and I'm talking about the ones who come to church *every single Sunday*. When we call upon them to coherently express the biblical and theological content of the faith, it's as if the connecting wires have been cut, the threads pulled loose from the tapestry. Part of the task of youth ministry is to restore those connections, to weave together the loose ends until *coherent* meaning emerges. This is where the youth-pastor-as-bard—as "speech weaver"—begins to make sense.

As I look back on my seven years in full-time youth ministry, the experiences that were the most formative for youth weren't the ones that required the largest sound systems or the most persuasive Christian apologetics, but the ones that made the strongest imaginative connections. They were the experiences that wove together the fragmented worlds of home, school, friendships, leisure, work, worship, storybooks, and scripture through engaging and nurturing young people's imaginations. Sure, those connections didn't happen the same way for *every* kid, *every* time—and the experiences certainly didn't fit into some sort of programmatic formula. Sometimes they made connections that were primarily visual; sometimes they were relational. Occasionally the experience inverted the students' expectations or made surprising and even startling connections that elicited strong emotional reactions. More often than not, they were unplanned and simply rose naturally from our work and worship.

If I could specifically identify some of those experiences, I'd say they tended to group themselves around the following elements: story, metaphor, parable, poetry, symbol, sacrament, pilgrimage, play, engagement with the arts (e.g., music, dance, visual art, etc.), service, and cross-cultural encounters. These elements seemed uniquely effective at connecting the dots between word and image, narrative and theology, community and kingdom, past and present, creed and practice. Sometimes they offered opportunities for engagement or synthesis; other times they prompted vision or empathy. Still other times they provided outlets for the imagination's creative response. Often they prompted all of these responses, much to my astonishment and delight. Again, I wish I could've provided a copy of *Redwall* for each of my confirmation campers!

The above list of nurturing experiences is not meant to be exhaustive or prescriptive; it merely highlights what I've sensed to be crucial elements that are often overlooked in predominantly entertainment-driven youth programming. These are the ways we nurture the imagination and help youth make meaningful connections. And, it's worth noting, all of them are present within both scripture and the worshiping community, in one form or another.

I wish I could vamp on all of these themes, but I'm afraid there's room in this book for only one—well, maybe two. You'll notice I put story at the top of the list. This is purposeful, obviously. Story is one of the most powerful ways we pattern our world and discover its meaningfulness. It goes beyond mere embellishment of a spiritual point to providing a nurturing form or substance for the God-hungry imagination, one that helps young people inhabit a narratable world. And story is what we'll explore in the next section of this book.

CLOSING THOUGHTS

The church's primary task in the spiritual formation of youth is to form them into the image of Christ. In this we are cocreators with God, nurturing young people's imaginations so they're able to make connections again, so a meaningful pattern emerges out of their otherwise incoherent lives. Through engagement, synthesis, vision, empathy, and creative response, we take the disconnected elements of their scattered worlds and weave them together. We say, "Remember how last week we heard about the Lion, how he invited Jill to come and drink from the stream? Does that remind you of anything? When are you invited to take a drink at home? with your friends? at church? Which drink will satisfy you forever? Let's take a sip of it right now. 'On the night when Jesus was arrested . . .'"

QUESTIONS AND EXERCISES

1. When do you feel tempted to think of youth ministry as formula rather than as formation? How might a healthy understanding of the imagination change the way you think about a young person's spiritual development?

2. Consider ways you've seen the Holy Spirit work through the imaginations of youth in your congregation. When you have seen engagement, meaningful synthesis, vision, empathy, or creative response?

3. Think of a young person in your church whose imaginative engagement with faith seems fragmented, unhealthy, or nonexistent. How can you help him or her make meaningful connections between home, school, friends, leisure, work, worship, and scripture?

IDEA FOR THE ROAD

With one or two other youth leaders, list the most formative experiences you've witnessed in youth ministry. Notice any themes that emerge, and then pray about how you might creatively incorporate some of those themes into your ministry this year.

FARE FOR THE IMAGINATION

For the story that shapes a child's universe also shapes the child—and by the child, the man thereafter. The memory of a burning fairy tale can govern behavior as truly as remembered fire will caution against fire forever.

—WALTER WANGERIN JR.[11]

PART 3

STORY

A young man sits in a packed college chapel, listening to an orchestra concert. Usually he's not the kind of person who enjoys orchestral performances, much less those assigned for class, but in this case he's riveted. The piece is a tribute to D-Day, and the cacophony of noise swells like a gun battle. He feels the chaos in his chest, an all-too-familiar turbulence that seems to echo his own spiritual confusion. All the intellectual doubts about faith that have arisen during his time at this landmark Christian institution are there in force, wave after wave of assault on the shores of his soul. The chaos swells, the battle rises to fever pitch, and then suddenly—a single melody sounds into an abrupt silence.

It plays not "Taps," as one might expect, but a simple line from the chorus of an old hymn: "It is well . . ." rings the plaintive tune, "with my soul . . . It is well, it is well with my soul."

There in the audience, with the echoes of war still humming in the walls, the young man puts his face in his hands and weeps. He weeps for the faith that carried him through childhood, a faith that is no longer his. He weeps for weariness, for longing, for the painful awareness that he can take no comfort from the simple words of the old hymn—words that are there behind the notes, rising up from distant childhood memories. All arguments have failed. All defenses of Christian truth have been thrown down. He is alone in the silence on the other side of chaos, and it is not well with his soul.

Later that summer the young man picks up a book. It's the fourth in a children's series about some British children who end up in a magical world called Narnia, ruled by a wonderful lion named Aslan. In this particular story, two of the kids have embarked on an adventure to save the lost prince of Narnia, and—along with their companion, a strange creature known as a Marsh-wiggle—they find themselves trapped in the Underland in the clutches of an evil witch. She puts them under a spell in which they forget all about their quest and begin to doubt the existence of Narnia and of Aslan himself. But just when all hope seems lost, the Marsh-wiggle rallies.

"Suppose we *have* only dreamed, or made up, all those things," the young man says in defiance. " . . . Then all I can say is . . . the made-up things seem a good deal more important than the real ones." He vamps on this theme for a while and then concludes, "I'm on Aslan's side even if there isn't any Aslan to lead it. I'm going to live as like a Narnian as I can even if there isn't any Narnia."[1] This breaks the witch's spell. He and the children go on to defeat the witch, save the prince, and escape the Underland back to the Narnia that was there all along.

The young man pauses in reading the story. Here is an argument he's never heard before—not for the existence of God, but for choosing God's side in spite of one's own existential doubts. The young man suddenly knows what must be done. The alternative is too grim, too Underlandish. He must choose God's side even if there isn't any God to lead it; he must live as much like the King as he can, even if there isn't any kingdom. Can he choose? He can, by God's grace. And he does.

—ⵗ—

The young man in the story is now my husband of ten years and a seminary student at Duke Divinity School. To this day he credits C. S. Lewis's *The Silver Chair* with helping him "buy the more enduring story" that is Jesus Christ, in spite of intellectual doubts. In the eleven years since choosing God's side, it hasn't been perfect, but it has been well, with Tom's soul.

The curious thing, from a spiritual formation standpoint, is that young Tom had everything going for him up to his moment of crisis. He had been raised by Christian parents and grandparents, was active in church and youth group, and was well-known on his high school campus as a Christian leader. He chose a Christian college so he could grow spiritually. But several things rattled his faith over time, which eventually brought him to the intellectual breaking point. And it wasn't his family, or his youth director, or his pastor, or even his girlfriend who brought him through it (though I was the one who suggested he pick up The Chronicles of Narnia for some light summer reading). It was a story. More specifically, it was a good story that pointed to the Great Story.

We youth ministers often hear about the importance of building ongoing relationships with youth in order to earn the right to speak into their otherwise fragmented lives. Most of the key adults they know are simply too busy to grace them with the dignity of attention, too fragmented themselves to listen to what youth are saying. When an adult takes them seriously, young people are validated. They're much more likely to pay attention to what that grown-up has to say, and they're more likely to stay connected to the church than if no adults in the congregation had taken the time to get to know them.

Relational ministry is certainly important—I've been both the recipient and giver of that kind of spiritual investment—but a word of caution as we enter this section on story. Relationship can only carry a youth ministry so far before it's disrupted by the transitional nature of youth ministry itself. Youth are forever joining and ditching us—blame sports or hormones or parental visitation rights, if you like. And we youth workers, notoriously, don't always stick around in the same job for long, at which point many of the kids we built relationships with tend to drift away from the church. Add to that those rogue elements of spiritual formation that don't fit the programmatic formula (such as a life-changing Bible camp with total strangers, or a Christian concert with kids from another church), and the relational ministry model becomes wobbly at best.

We and the youth may be here today and gone tomorrow, but no matter: the church's task in this hour is to impart "the more enduring story."

So what do I propose instead? Well, first I must make clear that I'm not proposing we ditch relationships: they're one of the most important elements of the church's ministry to youth. Rather, I caution against making relationships the primary foundation for our ministry. Because the truth is, we youth workers don't live forever. We won't be there eternally for these kids. If we impart anything of value, it should be more than just the impression of our personalities or memories of shared events; it should be the one thing that matters in all the world, the one thing that began before we got here and will continue long after we're gone: the story of Jesus Christ. "Remember," he told his friends, "I am with you always, to the end of the age" (Matt. 28:20). We and the youth may be here today and gone tomorrow, but no matter: the church's task in this hour is to impart "the more enduring story."

In the midst of doing so, we're also telling the smaller stories of our lives, of the church, of the communities in which we live. We share parables, testimony, insights from great literature, music, drama, film. We worship together through scripture and sacrament. We serve alongside one another. As youth workers, we offer numerous "story-moments" in the process of spiritual formation, moments that nurture the God-hungry imaginations of our students; and, like skilled bards, we weave those moments together into a coherent, meaningful narrative that continually points back to the gospel. This is how we help our young people inhabit a narratable world.

Our previous discussion explored the imagination's role in helping youth make connections between the church, the world, and their lives; which in turn is how they begin to understand why faith actually matters. Now we'll look at the content of faith itself: the nature and structure of the biblical narrative and the forms we use to tell it.

Somehow the church has forgotten what it knew for so long: story goes beyond simply illustrating some spiritual point or other; it gives form to content; it *incarnates meaning.* So if the youth minister is a bard whose interests go beyond mere entertainment or lecture, then he or she must understand the craft of story by having a solid grasp on its basic elements.

CHAPTER 4

WHAT IS STORY, AND WHY DOES IT WORK?

You tell a story because a statement would be
inadequate. When anybody asks what a story is
about, the only proper thing is to tell him to
read the story.

—Flannery O'Connor

Story has staying power. We remember the illustrations from
Sunday's sermon for months afterward, but by coffee hour we're
already struggling to recite the pastor's three main points,
despite various acronyms meant to help us. Youth in our Sunday
school class can repeat almost verbatim some obscure parable we
dramatized last year, and yet they forget the core doctrinal statement we taught last week. Why is this? Why does story stick with us
for so long? And what must we understand about it in order to
engage it effectively?

As with imagination, before we can understand why and how
story works, we must be clear on what story *is* and *is not*.

WHAT IS STORY?

I. STORY IS ABOUT TRUTH

"I'm writing a book for youth pastors on storytelling," I said to a friend. She looked at me sideways and then wisecracked, "So, you're instructing them how to lie?" I didn't laugh; I probably should have. She realized I wasn't amused, however, and immediately rearranged her features to look all serious and scholarly. *That's* when I laughed.

Her joke brings up an unfortunate misconception about story. No doubt you know dozens of people—including Christians—who put unswerving trust in their national news anchors but view literature and other forms of narrative, especially fiction, with suspicion. Despite our culture's current love affair with postmodern relativism ("what's true for you isn't necessarily true for me"), we still tend to think of journalism as true, while story—or rather, narrative in its various forms, whether fiction or memoir or film—is somehow false. Christians are especially lazy about these distinctions, which is why postmodern youth are often bewildered by how we talk, particularly when it comes to the biblical narratives. So let's get our semantics straight. Story does not equal fiction, much less "lies." It's the world we Christians inhabit as "people of the Book." We are story people.

All the great cultures of the world insist, and have always insisted, that story deals in truth. Its subject matter is human experience, and thus its aim is to ring true. I'd even go so far as to say that story often deals in truth more faithfully than journalism, which deals in facts—because facts can be manipulated, distorted, and ignored without the reader necessarily being aware. But a reader always knows when a narrative doesn't ring true, which is why storytellers are some of the hardest-working people you'll ever meet—J. R. R. Tolkien, author of *The Lord of the Rings*, being a case in point (it took him fourteen years to finish his epic fantasy!). While journalism gives us the bald details and lets us draw our own conclusions (technically speaking), story may include bald details of historical fact; but it also leaves out details that are irrelevant to the development of the main character(s) and basic theme(s). In short, while journalism purports to tell us what *happened*, story tells us what *happens*.[1]

Take the parables of Jesus, for example. Most of us would agree the parables are "true," and by this we mean more than simply that, at some point in history, Jesus told them. We mean they contain truth about who God is and who we are as human beings. They don't tell us what happened, as if Jesus were giving a journalistic account of a farmer he'd seen in the fields the day before; the parables tell us what happens. This is what human beings are like; this is what God is like; this is what the kingdom of God is like. Parables tell us what happens in the real world, and that's the heart of any good story.

> *Parables tell us what happens in the real world, and that's the heart of any good story.*

Truth is the aim of story. And though we must take into account the human author's subjectivity and personal slant, the best authors are those who tap universal longings and make connections to our real, lived humanity. The worst aren't those who attempt to deceive us about truth, as so many Christians seem to think, but those whose cultural perspective is so distorted by sin that truth is no longer recognizable either to the author or the reader.

The Da Vinci Code by Dan Brown is a negative case in point. Most likely the reason that story has captured the popular imagination is not because it purports to tell us what really *happened* in history. Rather, it unfortunately taps into what too often *happens* in human experience: the demythologizing of those heroes we once looked up to—be they politicians, sports figures, church leaders, or parents. Many of us at different points in our lives have felt betrayed by the church; that's what really happens in human experience, though it's not the only thing that happens. Whether or not the church has in fact buried the "truth" about Mary Magdalene becomes merely incidental to that deeper human experience of betrayal, at least for the average reader. And since our culture has also lost its sense of a reliable Christian metanarrative, there are few critical voices able to articulate a more persuasive tale than Brown's.

2. STORY IS MADE UP OF FOUR BASIC INGREDIENTS

At the risk of sounding like a ninth-grade English teacher, I feel it's important to make sure we're clear on what makes a story if we're to understand our role as bards and storytellers. Throughout this section I'll use an example most of us are familiar with, one I've mentioned numerous times already: Tolkien's *The Lord of the Rings*. In order to qualify as a story, a written, spoken, or performed narrative such as Tolkien's must include, at its most basic level, the following ingredients:

CHARACTER. Story almost always starts with a "who." This could be a historical figure, my mother, or some person I've just made up. It could even be an animal, a god, or an object that takes on anthropomorphic (human) qualities. In our example, it's an imaginary race of creatures known as Hobbits—who, for all their insistence on being different from humans, share our essential nature in everything but height (Hobbits are famously "three foot six"). In short, when it comes to story, we human beings are insatiably curious about other human beings, which is to say we're curious about ourselves. Story provides a mirror and a microscope that give us insight into what it means to be human, even when the central character is a modest Hobbit named Frodo Baggins in an imaginary world called Middle-earth. Frodo is our "who" and, as such, becomes a window into our own lives.

PLOT. Plot is a sequence of events involving our main character(s)—events driven by some kind of conflict, action, intrigue, or problem. The events aren't merely arbitrary but are somehow connected and eventually progress toward a crisis before their internal meaning or coherence is revealed/resolved (as in comedy) or overturned (as in tragedy). In Frodo's case, the plot is driven by quest: Frodo must go on a journey to destroy the Ring of Power before it falls into the hands of the Dark Lord Sauron, who would otherwise use the Ring to rule and destroy the world. Frodo's plot is in some moments a tragedy, where everything turns for the worse, but eventually the plot takes its comedic turn, and Middle-earth is saved—for now.

Plot generally follows a particular pattern, or prearranged sequence of events, sometimes called the *plotline* or *story arc*. Tales throughout the centuries and around the world have tended to fall into similar patterns that resonate with human experience. For example, psychologist Carl Jung identified stock characters (such as, say, the wicked stepmother) as "archetypes," while mythologist Joseph Campbell explored one mythic plot now known as the Hero's Journey.[2] This is precisely what Frodo Baggins embarks upon in *The Lord of the Rings*—what screenwriter Christopher Vogler calls the "mythic structure" of a hero's development, which includes such stages as call and refusal, testing and ordeal, reward and return, and, yes, even resurrection.[3]

Someone has said there are only, say, thirty basic plotlines in the whole world. In this view, every individual story is simply a retelling of an older story (though many postmoderns would disagree). Whatever the case, plot often takes a familiar narrative shape or pattern because that shape is inwardly satisfying to the human imagination. It feels "right"; it resonates with our deepest longings and desires—though often it can disrupt and frustrate those desires at the same time.

SETTING. Sometimes called *atmosphere*, *setting* is the backdrop against which the plot unfolds, or the boundaries of the narrative world. It may include the location or time period, such as the imaginary land of Middle-earth at the end of the Third Age; but it also includes the internal rules within the world of the story. So if it's a realistic novel, the characters shouldn't be able to fly. If it's a fantasy world, it must still adhere to its own internal rules: for example, dragons may fly in Middle-earth, but they'd better not sound like "an express train," as it says in the opening chapter of *The Fellowship of the Ring* (!). There are no modern machines in Middle-earth, much less a railway system; and Tolkien was forever irritated by this slip.

Tolkien was also irritated that his friend C. S. Lewis included Father Christmas in *The Chronicles of Narnia*, as if the Christ child had been born on the Narnian side of the wardrobe rather than the other way around—in which case, who is this Aslan figure, and why is he necessary? Such glitches in setting, unless carefully attended to, can bump a reader or hearer out of the story. (Lewis, for the record, didn't see any problem with throwing all kinds of myths, legends, and Christian elements into the Narnian pot; and most of his child readers eat it up.)

TONE. Tone is the narrative's unique voice and attitude, often determined by the narrator's own voice (as distinct from the author's) as well as by the intended audience and narrative form (more on form later). Tone is where some readers struggle with Tolkien's story, because his voice or attitude tends to shift from section to section. For example, the beginning of *The Lord of the Rings* is lighthearted and often silly, much like the tone of its prequel, *The Hobbit* (which is considered a children's book); but eventually Tolkien realized this new story was much bigger and more intense than he expected. So by book 2 his tone shifts to high epic prose; at this point many readers lose interest, while the rest become lifelong Middle-earth junkies.

> *Tone is where journalism and story go their separate ways.*

Tone is how the narrator expresses his or her own personality, which is why we might forgive a memoir for having a particular slant but can't forgive a newspaper article for doing the same. Tone is where journalism and story go their separate ways; because while in journalism the writer is supposed to be invisible, in story someone tells us what's happening, and the storyteller's tone often determines how we receive what is being said.

Character, plot, setting, and tone. Obviously, this is not all that story must include, but these are the basic ingredients. File them away, because we'll return to them later and discuss how and why they matter for ministry!

3. STORY FOLLOWS A BASIC THEMATIC STRUCTURE OR PATTERN, ALSO KNOWN AS FORM

I want to be sure we don't confuse *sequence of events* (plot) with *thematic content* (form). Plot is a pattern of events; form is a pattern of themes. For Tolkien's narrative, the plot or pattern of events is that of quest, while the form or pattern of themes is that of fairy tale. Fairy tale explores the supernatural, the "other world" that exists beyond our ordinary, everyday life. For Tolkien, fairy tale as a form allowed him to explore a specifically Christian understanding of the supernatural. He wrote, "In *The Lord of the Rings* the conflict is not basically about 'freedom', though that is naturally involved. It is about God, and His sole right to divine honour."[4] We may not immediately glean this from Tolkien's stories, but this is precisely the strength of form: it embodies themes; it doesn't necessarily state them overtly.

Just as it's easy to confuse form with plot, it's easy to confuse form with *style*. While form is the thematic structure of the narrative, style is the particular artistic flavor or flair the author gives to the language and tone. We see the distinction in housing construction: form is the structure and shape of the foundation and frame; style is the choice of siding (aluminum, cedar shake) or the color of the door. For every house the form is essentially the same: a foundation, walls, roof, windows, doors, ventilation, and protective siding of some sort. And yet each individual house is uniquely different in style depending on the artistic temperament and preferences of its inhabitants. The same is true with story. While the story has an overall thematic structure—form—it also includes those embellishments that mark the author's unique creative style. For Tolkien, the complex and lyrical nature of the many languages he invented lends his story a unique and unforgettable style that many fantasy writers have since tried to emulate.

Different forms have different strengths as well as require different restrictions on what is and isn't included in the narrative. C. S. Lewis's essay "Sometimes Fairy Stories May Say Best What's to Be Said" sums up the issue quite well: there were certain themes Lewis wished to explore, and he found fairy tale to be the best form for doing so with children, hence The Chronicles of Narnia. The meaning he was attempting to express or explore is incarnate in the stories' form as fairy tale. In other books he turned to other forms—such as satire, memoir, allegory, poetry, and myth—to explore other, albeit similar, themes. As every writer will tell you, some forms work better than others for certain themes or audiences. (Few writers have Lewis's flexibility, however.)

The form of a story is where its essential meaning begins to emerge (and also, not incidentally, where one begins to sense whether or not it's a well-crafted story). "Meaning and narrative shape bear significantly on each other," wrote the late theologian Hans Frei[5]; or, as Flannery O'Connor put it, "In the act of writing, one sees that the way a thing is made, controls and is inseparable from the whole meaning of it. The form of a story gives it meaning which any other form would change."[6] To ignore a story's form is to risk missing what the story means, and this goes for both hearer and teller. I can't stress this point strongly enough for youth pastors in particular and the church in general, which is why we'll return to it in the next few chapters when we discuss the implications of story for ministry.

WHY DOES STORY WORK?

We've already recognized that story "works"; it has staying power. That's because, through its basic ingredients (character, plot, setting, tone), *story provides a satisfying pattern for the imagination to grab hold of.* And through its thematic structure (form), story incarnates meaning, embodies content, rather than confronting the hearer's reason with propositional argument. It presents itself in nonthreatening ways so the hearer's defenses are down; it slips past those "watchful dragons" and makes connections that are not easily forgotten.

Given the above issues, we can safely assert that story has the potential to influence spiritual formation. It does this by facilitating the five activities we've identified as crucial to imaginative health:

engagement, synthesis, vision, empathy, and creative response. Again, I think of my correspondent in Tokyo whose life was profoundly touched by reading *The Lord of the Rings* as a teenager. His imagination was first engaged with—or, shall we say, gripped by—an epic narrative that was like nothing he'd ever heard before. As he processed and synthesized the story's themes, he began to sense that in real life, as in Tolkien's fantasy world, good and evil are at war. He envisioned what it might mean for him personally to choose the good side, though he wasn't quite sure what that looked like yet. He connected empathetically with the character of Sam, Frodo's companion on the journey, who cries out a kind of prayer when facing the forces of evil. And this young teenager began to pray that prayer himself as a way to creatively respond to the longing in his own heart. So with his imagination firing on all cylinders, he then went off to the Billy Graham event and found that the worlds of scripture, Middle-earth, and his own life were strands woven together into a larger tapestry expressing none other than the image of Jesus Christ. And this was only the beginning.

Obviously, story doesn't do this every time. That's the Holy Spirit's business. But it does create an atmosphere in which a number of formative experiences are possible. Let's take a look at a few of those.

INTIMACY

Story creates a connection between the teller and the hearer(s). It involves an implicit "we" community, such as a grandfather and child cuddled close, reading together, or the "I" inserted into the narrative of a fairy tale. Our young people feel connected to the narrator of a story in ways they're usually not with their immediate circle (especially with adults). Somehow the narrator is giving of himself or herself in deeper and more vulnerable ways than in regular discourse. Writes Native American storyteller Ray Buckley:

> A child relates storytelling . . . to human contact, and that
> contact becomes as much a part of the story as the story
> itself. As adults, we experience storytelling in much the

same fashion. Isn't it interesting that in many cultures, storytelling is viewed as a form of touch?[7]

Shared stories also create a sense of community, fellowship. Years later our young people can turn to each other and say, "Remember when . . . ?"

IDENTITY

If we want the next generation to know where they came from and thus who they are, we tell them stories so they won't forget. Then they pass the stories on to the generation after them, and so it goes. Story expresses the beliefs and values of a people by incarnating those values in unforgettable images rather than abstract statements. It preserves cultural memory and gives the hearer a sense of his or her identity within community. Buckley writes, "Within our stories are contained elements of our cultures that we wish to transmit to other generations. Our primary purpose is not to entertain but to continue culture."[8] Story shapes worldview, which in term shapes self-understanding or identity.

WONDER

If imagination, as we've said, is the "region of discovery," story is the wardrobe door, sending our young people "further in" and "still further in" to possibilities and ideas they've never dreamed. It expands their capacity to wonder; it excites their natural curiosity so they want to know what happens next. In a postmodern world, where awe has all but disappeared from daily experience, story restores a sense of astonishment that the universe is much larger—and humans much smaller—than our students thought. To quote one of my favorite literary characters: "This must be a simply enormous wardrobe!"[9]

WORLD BUILDING

Story satisfies a teenager's natural creative drive because it forces her to be an active participant in imaginatively building the world of the story. She creates the story along with the storyteller; her imagination borrows elements from her known world and builds new worlds. She takes enormous satisfaction in the creative process, particularly when that process rises to the level of myth making and speaks to universal longings and desires.

PLAY

Closely connected to world building is play: the suspension of everyday activities for the sheer fun of invention and for release, without any consideration for the results. Story may have a "purpose," but it may not. For example, teens often ask me, "What's the point of Tolkien's *The Lord of the Rings*? Is he making a political protest, a religious statement, a moral argument?" No, as Tolkien was quick to insist, there is no point—or at least, he didn't set out to argue or promote anything. What launched his story was the sheer delight he took in inventing languages, from which he then invented cultures and people and a history to go with it all. If there is a point to the epic narrative, it's that God can be glorified in our creative play. Story is one important way this happens.

TIMELESSNESS

Our students need a break from the daily grind, a chance to touch eternity. This longing for timelessness draws them to stories, because a good story (and good art in general) sends them into what some theologians have called *kairos*, an ancient Greek word appropriated to mean time in all its fullness: quality time. Its counterpoint is *chronos*, the everlasting tick of the clock, the inevitable approach of sunset, the driving force behind the world's frantic activity. By contrast, writes Madeleine L'Engle, "in *kairos* we are completely un-self-conscious and yet paradoxically far more real than we can ever be when we are constantly checking our watches for chronological time."[10] Story has a beginning, middle, and end, giving our young people a sense of connection to the past, present, and future; it makes them capable of experiencing both memory and expectation rather than just the "tyranny of the urgent."

ENCHANTMENT

Story temporarily enchants young listeners, weaving a spell that freezes time like the castle of Sleeping Beauty or the village of Brigadoon. They lose all sense of place and even of self. Writes Tolkien, "Small wonder that *spell* means both a story told, and a formula of power over living men."[11] (And, not incidentally, *spell* also means a break from work, as in "Come sit with me for a spell.") When the world is enchanted, time is of no consequence. Story—particularly fantasy and fairy tale—reminds our young people that behind the relentless tick of the clock by which they live their busy, "purpose-driven" lives, is the unhurried, unperturbed pace of that other kingdom, the kingdom of God's eternity. No wonder the gospel as story is more than just the "good news" but the "good spell"!

TRANSCENDENCE

Story lifts our young listeners out of themselves, offering the chance for self-forgetfulness—a much-needed gift to a generation of self-obsessed materialists. As my friend Claire, a young seminary student, told me, "My instructors keep saying, 'Put yourself into the Gospels. Find yourself there.' And I keep saying, 'But I don't want to put myself into the Gospels. I want to *lose* myself for once.'" C. S. Lewis said it this way: "In reading great literature I become a thousand men and yet remain myself. . . . I transcend myself; and am never more myself than when I do."[12] Story gives our young people the gift of un-self-consciousness, even as it returns them to themselves with new awareness.

RESONANCE

Walter Wangerin Jr. writes, "To identify well with a major character in a story *is* to identify oneself."[13] Story resonates with our teenagers' human experience, like a bell that hums faintly when another bell has been struck nearby. There is a startled flash of recognition when a story seems to speak directly to their unique situation even as it expresses a universal longing. As one of C. S. Lewis's students says in the movie *Shadowlands*, "We read to know we're not alone."

SUBVERSION

The meaning of a story is not expressed overtly in trite little morals or platitudes—otherwise, as Flannery O'Connor says, "you can be sure the story is not a very good one."[14] Story famously subverts its themes or overall messages by keeping them beneath the surface, which is why the hearer's defenses are down and he or she is more willing to listen. In the most subversive stories, such as parables, the storyteller may even choose to hide or obscure as much or more than he reveals. Subversion allows for truth to sink in slowly over time—delayed epiphany. It puts great faith in the hearer's imagination to keep mulling things over long after "The End."

MYSTERY

To enter the realm of story is to enter the realm of mystery, to embrace impossibilities through what Coleridge called the imagination's "willing suspension of disbelief."[15] Story affirms that not everything in the universe can or must be explained propositionally; the loose ends of story aren't always neatly tied together, because neither are the loose ends of our lives. "Life can bear only so much reality," says poet and pastor Calvin Miller. "We need the mysteries to live. In every message that I preach, I call [people], not to scientifically reasonable faith, but to a faith which gains its power through stories."[16]

CLOSING THOUGHTS

Needless to say, most of the experiences listed in this chapter are, by and large, missing from the lives of our young people—which is why (I suspect) this generation flooded movie theaters for three successive years when *The Lord of the Rings* hit the box office. It's also worth noting these experiences are generally absent from most entertainment-driven or lecture-oriented youth programming. When was the last time you heard a long passage from a novel read aloud during Sunday school or worship? Or how about the last time a youth pastor subverted his or her "talk" through satire or parable rather than proof texting the six main points?

Yet the experiences I've described are things that nurture the imagination and give story its unique staying power, in addition to the satisfying shape or pattern of the narrative itself. As a church, we must take these aspects of story seriously if we are to help youth inhabit a narratable world. Which is (you guessed it!) the subject of our next discussion.

QUESTIONS AND EXERCISES

1. When have you observed Christians confuse *story* with *fiction* or even *lies*? What implications might this have for the way they approach scripture and worship?

2. In what ways has a story (or stories) influenced your own spiritual formation? What characteristic of the story had such an effect on you (resonance, mystery, wonder, timelessness, etc.), and why?

3. When have you experienced how the narrative shape or form of a story influences the imagination as well as its expression of meaning? How might this understanding of form influence the way you handle stories in youth ministry?

IDEA FOR THE ROAD

At your next youth gathering, instead of giving the customary "talk" or "devotion," consider reading a longish passage from a novel such as *The Silver Chair*, by C. S. Lewis, or Anne Tyler's *Saint Maybe*. You may need to set the tone beforehand by gathering the youth in a circle or lighting a candle. Refrain from explaining the passage afterwards, if possible—although if discussion ensues, encourage questions that begin with "I wonder . . .?"[17]

FARE FOR THE IMAGINATION

Children have an instinctive aversion to leaving anything out of a story. Indeed, it is children's passionate belief in the existence of a master narrative that makes them the heirs of the kingdom.

—GREGORY WOLFE[18]

CHAPTER 5

WHAT STORY ARE WE TELLING?

If I'm gonna be a preacher one day, I gotta
know the Bible front to back. I mean, you can't
help nobody if you can't tell 'em the right story.
—JOHNNY CASH'S BROTHER, JACK,
IN THE MOVIE *WALK THE LINE*

Earlier I mentioned my friend who serves as the youth director
of a mainline church that no longer holds a Good Friday service because it's "too depressing." Needless to say, when my
friend, out of protest, showed Mel Gibson's *The Passion of the Christ*
at a youth retreat on Good Friday, it was the first time most of those
kids had ever heard the Crucifixion story. Not only were they
touched on a personal level, but they found themselves woven into
the larger story of historic Christianity, possibly for the first time.

Her church's loss of the Passion has sad implications for more
than just the youth ministry. It affects the congregation's approach to
the inhabitable narratives of both scripture and worship as a whole.
Now there are huge chunks of the Gospels that must strenuously be
avoided, and the worshiping body no longer lives within the liturgical (that is to say, narrative) arc of the church year. It misses what a

literary person like me would consider to be the climax, the ultimate crisis point, of the entire plot. And if you miss *that*, I'm not sure that what you have technically qualifies as a story, much less a "narratable world." I'd even question whether it qualifies as Christianity.

And yet the truth is, every church has a story—or rather, a whole mess of competing stories. Even when the biblical-liturgical narrative is fully operative in the life of a congregation, there are all kinds of competing narratives floating around, stories that have seeped in from popular culture and bear little resemblance to historical Christianity. Here we think of *Soul Searching*'s "Moralistic Therapeutic Deism," for example—where religion merely makes you a better person, and God is a Cosmic Therapist. Other "stories" might include the American Dream, power politics, and the Left Behind series on the one hand; or the Jesus Seminar, inclusivism at all costs, and the Gnostic Gospels on the other. You get the point. We can hardly walk anywhere in the average American sanctuary without bumping into somebody's story. The question isn't, which story is true? but, how do we put the kibosh on this kind of silliness so we can raise up a generation of genuine Christ followers?

The cure for competing narratives is nothing more or less than the Apostles' Creed. Yes, I'll say that again: the creed is our story, succinctly stated. Take it as a political statement if you like, but I'm coming at it mainly from a literary perspective. As any writer will tell you, if an author can't tell an editor what her story is about in a few sentences, then that editor has every right to question whether the writer really knows her stuff—and, more importantly, whether the story is worth backing. This doesn't mean the full-blown story itself won't embellish and enrich the author's succinct summary, but it does mean the storyteller had better fulfill the promises of and stay accountable to that summary. If the author can't do that, her editor has every right to back out of the whole deal. And if you think I'm merely being cute or clever, may I remind you that backing out is exactly what our young people are doing from the church. That's their editorial comment.

The Apostles' Creed is our summary, or as author Kathleen Norris puts it, "an admirably compact form of storytelling."[1] It's not the full-blown story of scripture or of everyday life in the community of faith, but it isn't simply a "grocery list" of beliefs, either. It is primarily *narrative* in content, language, and form rather than theological (unlike so many of the "statements of faith" posted on evangelical Web sites)—which gives the creed major brownie points as far as the imagination is concerned. Its narrative shape provides something substantial for the imagination to grasp hold of.

Now, certainly it's tempting to complain about what *isn't* included in the creedal narrative, such as the huge swaths of scripture that go unsung. I hardly need remind us that the summary is no substitute for the story. An editor doesn't want just the author's one-page proposal. But the creed's essential theme is the same as that of the scriptures themselves, which is to offer us a "faithful portrait" of God in Christ.[2] It describes in the pithiest terms possible, not only the narrative pattern we live into as Christ's followers but our uniqueness in a pluralistic world of competing narratives.

I'm not advocating that we recite the creed every time we gather for worship or discuss faith with teenagers. I *am* saying we keep its narrative structure always in the back of our minds as we minister. We gauge every "story-moment" according to the normative world of the creed. Will this moment help clarify essential themes of the narrative we live by? Have we missed any vital chapters in our efforts to develop those themes we particularly like while ignoring the ones we don't, to our peril?

The example of my friend's church highlights just what happens when the creedal structure of the church's overarching story is dismissed as irrelevant. A whole generation of children and youth are growing up without hearing that Jesus "suffered under Pontius Pilate, was crucified, died and was buried"—and most certainly without knowing he "descended to the dead" (which is too bad, since this is how most of them feel every morning before school). What they've been given instead is sentimental therapy, which in no way prepares them to suffer alongside another human being for the sake of Christ, to recognize Christ in the midst of pain, to pursue the purposeful descent of a downwardly mobile lifestyle in solidarity with the oppressed. (And in the midst of all this, I can't help wondering:

Do contemporary churches really think they can abandon historic, creedal Christianity while simultaneously empowering a new generation of champions for missions or social justice?)

As privileged Americans who constitute the demographic of most mainline and evangelical churches, if we don't let ourselves go to the darkest place of Good Friday, how can our young people possibly appreciate the light of Easter? It's like Jesus' statement about the one who is forgiven little: we have suffered little, therefore we rejoice little. Easter remains merely lovely, like a stroll through a garden in our Sunday best, as opposed to the way a shipwrecked man feels when his feet finally touch the shore. "For the loss of the Great Story is a pastoral loss," writes David Mills. "It is the loss of the healing word we have to say to those who suffer. It is like forgetting the formula for the cure for cancer."[3]

> *The church is the narratable world we're inviting youth into; it's both narrator and homeland.*

Beyond reclaiming and telling the Great Story, the church must, as Robert Jenson has said, *be* the story. The church is the narratable world we're inviting youth into; it's both narrator and homeland. Gregory Wolfe writes:

> If there is an imaginative challenge for our time, it is to hear and transmit the still small voice of divine authority amid the cacophony of individualism and power politics, and to show that the astonishment we feel in the presence of that voice will lead not toward oppression, but toward true community.[4]

In the end, there *is* a normative story that we live into as a church: the story God is telling through scripture, as summarized in the words of the creed. And rather than tearing us apart, it provides the loom upon which the disconnected elements of our lives are woven together into a true community that images forth Christ to the world.

NARRATIVE INGREDIENTS OF SCRIPTURE

In the previous chapter we considered what story is and is not. We explored its basic ingredients, the importance of form, and why story "works"—why it has such staying power in the imagination. Now let's consider what specific implications this has for the church's ministry to youth, particularly in our understanding of scripture as story.

The Bible *is* story as we defined it in the previous chapter, containing all the basic ingredients and qualities needed: character, plot, setting, tone, and form. It is "not a theological outline with proof texts attached. It is an anthology of literature."[5] Contrary to the cavalier attitude many pastors and religious educators take on this point, the Bible's narrative ingredients do matter for how we understand what's happening in a given book or chapter, along with how these individual stories fit together. Who is telling this Bible story? And to whom is the author telling it? Who is the story about, and why? Where is this whole thing headed, anyway?

CHARACTER. Within the many narratives of scripture, each individual story's main foci may vary from book to book; but the overarching theme, as we've already said, is to create a "faithful portrait" of the character of God in Christ. The Gospels in particular "are portraits, narratives that give us renderings," says Richard Hays.[6]

A failure on the part of both liberals and conservatives is to present the Gospel narratives as merely illustrations of some theological "point" rather than carefully crafted renderings of a unique character in history, with certain aspects highlighted more than others. We're especially lazy about this in youth ministry. The story becomes secondary to the theological or cultural topic we want to discuss. I'm indebted to the writings of Hans Frei for the reminder that Jesus is not some example or metaphor about an abstract principle, such as love or grace: he is a person, and the stories in the

Gospels are told in order to paint a "faithful portrait" of his character. Their purpose is for us to know a Person, not a "point."

So here's an exercise to try with your students in Sunday school or confirmation sometime. Show them a student's senior portrait in which the subject is wearing, say, a soccer uniform and holding a ball. Obviously this is not a candid snapshot snatched in the midst of his everyday life. A journalist didn't walk by and catch him sitting on a stepladder in his uniform, surrounded by trophies all facing in the same direction. Rather, the photo is a carefully crafted portrait meant to emphasize certain things about his character that are most important to him and to the people who know and love him. And even though it's carefully crafted, it's meant to faithfully represent or render who the kid is. So is the picture "true"? Is it "faithful"? Yes and yes. The same can be said of the Gospels in particular and the Bible in general, broadly speaking, of course. Each unique story is important, and each is attempting to highlight some aspect of God's character that helps us know God better. Together they make up a portrait gallery of distinct renderings, some beautiful, some strange, all necessary.

PLOT. The Bible-as-story contains many interweaving plots, but from those narratives emerges the traditional story arc of creation, rebellion, exile, redemption, and return. This may sound alarmingly linear or "reductionistic" (a favorite term of my husband's seminary friends whenever someone tries to express anything in simplistic terms), but closer scrutiny reveals just how cyclical and organic this story arc is. Consider the narrative of the Exodus, for example. First, through Moses God brings about (creates) a new people who are free from slavery in Egypt. Then they rebel against God in the wilderness and wander in exile for decades. Yet even in the midst of their rebellion, God redeems them through merciful provision, covenant, and commandment. Eventually they return to the land of their forefathers.

And round and round it goes, sometimes rehearsed in smaller stories like Samson, sometimes played out in the larger dramas, such as David's reign and lineage. And all the while the wheel is turning inevitably toward the birth of Jesus. "I am about to do a new thing," God says in Isaiah 43:19, "now it springs forth, do you not perceive it?" The people rebel against this new thing; Christ redeems them by paying the ultimate price; and now, as his people we live into the promise of his coming reign. Creation, rebellion, redemption, return.

This is putting it rather simplistically, of course, and yet we can't forget how important a concise plot summary is for giving us (and our students) a healthy grasp of the story's general pattern, the satisfying and meaningful shape it offers the imagination. This is a Divine Comedy we're talking about, not some tragic Greek drama or episode from reality TV. Again, we can turn to the Apostles' Creed for a pithy expression of the plot. What happens when we ignore certain key episodes, such as the Passion? The narrative cycle is broken; the story degenerates into meaninglessness.

SETTING. It's easy for our young people to think of the biblical stories as taking place long, long ago and far, far away, and thus having no real relevance for our contemporary situation. Chalk up this attitude to their need for cultural "relevance" or to their inveterate "chronological snobbery," if you like; I think it points to an underlying nervousness that any of this Bible stuff might have anything to do with me. C. S. Lewis as a young man thought of God as a kind of "transcendental Interferer,"[7] and I don't think he was the last one to think this way. And yet "interfering" in young people's lives is exactly what God has done and continues to do; and this takes place right now, right here, in this particular story, in this particular setting.

In speaking of the creed, Dorothy Sayers writes, "All over the world, thousands of times a day, Christians recite the name of a rather undistinguished Roman pro-consul [Pontius Pilate]—not in execration . . . but merely because that name fixes within a few years the date of the death of God."[8] This story happened at a particular time in a particular place to a particular people—a concept that theologians often call the "scandal of particularity." The setting itself becomes a kind of a shock. This is especially true when it suddenly hits our young people that the story's not over. As a theologian friend of mine once cheerfully told a roomful of high school students, "We are chapter 3,647 of the book of Acts." The backdrop for this ongoing story is now, not several millennia ago; and our teenagers have a part to play.

TONE. A leading youth ministry expert makes this bald statement: "The Bible is propaganda."[9] The weird thing is that he says this immediately after pronouncing that the Bible is God's story! My response? The Bible cannot be both great literature *and* religious propaganda: the Bible is *story*. It's an artistically rendered narrative on which there is occasional commentary, which then informs our systems, doctrines, or causes. Specifically, the Bible's overall tone or voice is that of a *"realistic narrative"*[10]—that is to say, written about real events—which means it includes stuff that doesn't always fit or make sense within a theological framework, unlike the sentimental and allegorical schlock that constitutes most religious propaganda.

The Bible-as-narrative takes precedence over our attempts to express Christian belief in propositional or abstract terms, which is to say the stories come first. Sure, the authors have a driving theme they're trying to articulate: this is called communication. Writes Flannery O'Connor:

> Unless the novelist [or storyteller] has gone utterly out of his mind, his aim is still communication, and communication suggests talking inside a community. . . . The isolated imagination is easily corrupted by theory, but the writer inside his community seldom has such a problem.[11]

The biblical writers were not "isolated imaginations": they were writing within and for a community, not a "cause."

If the thrust of scripture can be boiled down into an abstract point, then what could possibly be the purpose of story except as a very shabby attempt to coat the message to make it easier to swallow? If the Bible is merely propaganda, then it would ring more false than true because it would be unable to stand on its own legs as a narrative without some kind of dogmatic message behind it. But it does stand on its own legs: the Gospel narratives in particular. The story is appealing–in fact, enchanting. If all it's designed to do is embellish or illustrate a point, then its essential nature is lost. Postmoderns must have the opportunity to experience the story as a story without the gospel being continually reduced to mere message.

You might try exploring this aspect of narrative with your high school students after a shared mission experience or other significant event. If each of them were to tell a story of his or her experience, could the students really boil it down to one main point? My guess is that, in different renderings of the same story–depending on the audience or their reflections since it happened–the students would highlight certain themes they hadn't necessarily explored in previous retellings. Not to mention, each individual student would approach his or her rendering of the same experience differently than the others.

The hunt for the "moral of the story" ultimately strips the story of its essential tone, which means it runs the danger of no longer qualifying as a story at all. It's now either straight journalism or straight propaganda, and is nothing so remotely mysterious and beautiful as scripture.

THE IMPORTANCE OF FORM

Last summer I heard a guest speaker preach at a large and distinguished university chapel (ahem). She was speaking about her struggles with scripture back when she was a seminarian, particularly regarding the two very different creation narratives in Genesis 1 and 2. "But which one is true?" she wailed, and all of the distinguished-looking people around me chuckled sympathetically. I was hard-pressed not to roll my eyes. Maybe it's because I've been a literary geek all my life, but the question strikes me as ridiculous. The issue isn't which story is *true* but which one is *poetry*.

Even more important than the biblical author's tone is the narrative form the author has chosen to tell the story. Form is the story's thematic structure, selected for the meaning it conveys as well as for its pertinence to the intended audience and other considerations.

Different books of the Bible are written in different forms, such as realistic narrative, dream or vision, poem or lyric, epistle, and parable. As we already discussed, form determines what does and does not get included, and this is important for understanding what's going on in scripture at any given moment.

Let's go back to the preacher's frustration with the creation stories. A brief analysis of the literary structure of Genesis 1 reveals a pattern and wordplay that lands it squarely within the tradition of Hebraic poetry (of which there isn't a rhyming variety as we might think of it), which means there are lots of things left unsaid because they don't fit the criteria for that kind of poem. Likewise, the literary structure of Genesis 2 follows another kind of form altogether—prose narrative, which gives it a unique flexibility and fluidity that opens up all kinds of doors for things like dialogue. The issue has nothing to do with which story is true or false: it has to do with form. Understanding this has profound implications for how we teach and preach the scriptures, particularly with youth.

> *When engaging youth with the Bible-as-story, we must be wary of our impulse to "clarify" what's happening in a given narrative.*

Form incarnates meaning. The poetry of Genesis 1 is intentionally structured and repetitive, with a kind of simple elegance that is both startling and satisfying. What does this tell us about creation itself, about God, about the human response to, say, the stars or the sunrise? The poem's very form embodies meaning that isn't easy to parse from the poem itself. The same goes for the prose narrative in Genesis 2. Writes Hans Frei, "A great theme in literature of the novelistic type, like a pattern in a historical sequence, cannot be paraphrased by a general statement. To do so would approach reducing it to meaninglessness."[12]

When engaging youth with the Bible-as-story, we must be wary of our impulse to "clarify" what's happening in a given narrative, to explain "what John is getting at" or "what Matthew is trying to say" or "what Paul really means here."[13] I've been guilty of this more times than I care to admit, and I'm not alone. This is both a liberal and a conservative impulse, and you can tell what kind of church you're in by the language used to describe what the authors "really meant."

Writes Wesley Kort, "The narrative form itself, therefore, provides unity amidst the plurality of critical voices."[14] The one voice we want our young people to hear is that of the author—or, should we say, the Author.

> ~
> *The one voice we want our young people to hear is that of the author—or, should we say, the Author.*
> ~

Again, it might be interesting to explore the issue with high school students who have just returned from a mission trip. Invite some of them to try to describe their experience through poetry or song; invite others to do so through third-person prose narrative, still others through first-person letter, and so on. What happens? Things get left out of a lyric because of its structural and linguistic limitations, while prose can elaborate. And yet the language of a song is more memorable because of, say, its internal rhymes or pithy metaphors, while prose is primarily functional. Meanwhile, a letter is a different thing altogether: it gives far more of the author's thoughts, carrying perhaps more emotional freight than the rest. So which one is "true"? Silly question, really; and my guess is, your students are smart enough to catch on.[15]

One final thought on this point. Taking form seriously is yet another corrective to the concept of the Bible as "propaganda." As Ellen Davis says, "The reward for learning to listen to the Bible on its own terms is that a more spacious world opens to us."[16] The last thing I want is for my students to be on their guard about what this or that biblical author is selling. Instead I want to invite them into a "more spacious world" with few preconceived ideas about what they'll find there. Writes C. S. Lewis, "No poem will give up its secret to a reader who enters it regarding the poet as a potential deceiver, and determined not to be taken in. We must risk being taken in, if we are to get anything."[17] It's a risk I'm willing to help youth take.

WHY THE BIBLE-AS-STORY "WORKS"

One of the primary ways "a more spacious world opens to us" through scripture is by offering formative experiences that nurture the imagination. The Bible-as-story works. It works in all the ways that story itself works: in offering transcendence, identity, intimacy, timelessness, wonder, and so forth, on down the list from chapter 4. Let's look at one in particular: enchantment.

As I already mentioned, the gospel is both *evangelium* (the good news) and *god-spel* (the good story, or the good word). It's spellbinding all by itself without the need for explanation or embellishment—a point many of us in the church have long forgotten, if we ever knew it. I offer this example from an inner-city ministry I participated in during my undergraduate days.

Every Easter the coordinator of our weekly kids' club in the housing projects on Chicago's south side invited the volunteers and children to a banquet. There were never enough chairs to go around, so in this particular instance I ended up with a little girl named Kiki on my lap. All around us was pure chaos, but Kiki, dressed in her Easter best, sat primly eating cake. Spontaneously I asked, "Kiki, do you know why we celebrate Easter? Has anyone told you the story?" She shook her head. So I began: "Once there was a man named Jesus"—"Baby Jesus!" she said, and I nodded—"That's right: Baby Jesus. He grew up to be a man who went around healing people and telling them about God . . ." And I told the whole story, more or less, including how the angry people sentenced Jesus to death and killed him, but how death has no power over God, and so forth. She listened, riveted, her cake uneaten.

When I was done, she said the last thing I expected: "Tell it again." So I did. When I got to the end that time, she pointed to her friend in the next chair and said, "Tell her." So I said, "Why don't you help me?" and we told the story together.

There are bad stories and good stories, bad spells and good

spells. The gospel, as we've already said, is the "good spell." It enchants even as it invites, confronts, and repels. Sure, the biblical narratives are given to us as texts; but they are also mysteriously more than texts. The trick is not imposing our theological agendas onto what that "more" means, but instead being faithful to telling the story as a story in whatever medium we are given or gifted, while trusting the Holy Spirit "to accomplish abundantly far more than all we can ask or imagine" (Eph. 3:20). There is a mystery here that defies explanation, that draws the young very near the borders of fairyland, of enchantment. It beckons them into the "more spacious world" of God's kingdom, where the usual rules have been rearranged, and one is never quite certain what will happen next.

"Yet for all its confusion and wildness," Frederick Buechner assures us, "it is a world where the battle goes ultimately to the good, who live happily ever after, and where in the long run everybody, good and evil alike, becomes known by his true name."[18]

CLOSING THOUGHTS

Often I hear youth workers insist that our job is to "bring the Bible to life"—but I find this concept to be borderline heretical. The Word of God is "living and active," Hebrews 4:12 asserts, "sharper than any two-edged sword." And on the inside cover of my Bible, I once scribbled this quote attributed to Martin Luther: "The Bible is alive, it speaks to me; it has feet, it runs after me; it has hands, it lays hold of me." What kind of hubris makes us think we must "bring the Bible to life" in order to preach or teach effectively? The Bible is alive; it is our students who are dead and must be resurrected. Story stirs the sleeping; scripture raises the dead.

We've forgotten how to humbly interact with a story on its own terms; we've lost the ability to wonder, especially when it comes to stories of human encounters with divine power. So have our young people. As a church, how do we restore that sense of wonder? By restoring our sense of the Bible as story, both for us and for the youth we serve; and by surrendering to the work of the Holy Spirit in and through this text that is mysteriously more than text.

In the next section we'll consider what happens when the community of faith intentionally embodies that story through the art of storytelling.

QUESTIONS AND EXERCISES

1. What story (or stories) is your church telling? How closely do those stories sync with historic, biblical Christianity? What implications does this have for your church's youth ministry?

2. What, if anything, strikes you about the concept of scripture as a "faithful portrait" of the character of God in Christ? How might that be helpful as you facilitate young people's engagement with the Bible?

3. How easy is it to ignore the formative, even enchanting, nature of the Bible-as-story? What might happen if youth workers were to approach scripture "on its own terms" instead of attempting to boil it down into some kind of "point"?

IDEA FOR THE ROAD

In the Lenten weeks leading up to Good Friday, facilitate a youth Bible study in which the group compares the separate Passion narratives. Consider together these questions:

- What would be missing if the Bible didn't include Matthew?
- How is John's thematic structure unique from the others?
- In what ways do each of the Gospels give us a different, yet still faithful, "portrait" of Jesus?

FARE FOR THE IMAGINATION

The idea behind reciting a creed is reasonably simple. If you do not say the right lines, you may not be in the right story. For example, if you don't hear the lines, "To be or not to be, that is the question," chances are you are not watching a performance of Hamlet.

—RICHARD A. LISCHER[19]

PART 4

STORYTELLING

Our songs and our stories do more than
persuade others that an order exists: they build
the house; they weave a world; they companion
our listeners into the experience of such
ordered cosmos.

—WALTER WANGERIN JR.

everal years ago I attended the Urbana student missions conference held every three years by Intervarsity Christian Fellowship.
Roughly twenty thousand young adults were there from all over
the world, and every day we worshiped together in a huge superdome. That year the planners arranged for a drama team to recite
each day's scripture passages from memory.[1] When a gray-haired
storyteller first walked onto the stage alone, without props or
prompts, and told that day's text with simple passion, the students

were astonished into a kind of awed silence. The next few times, they applauded in anticipation before he began. By day four, he hadn't even opened his mouth before they were on their feet with a roar of excitement; but this time he couldn't silence the crowd. With all the cheering, clapping, stomping, and whistling, a stranger would have thought it was a rock concert. When he finally calmed them down, the silence in the superdome was electrifying. Twenty thousand young people gripped by nothing but the words of Isaiah and then erupting with wild applause again when it was finished—when was the last time your kids did that in church?

When was the last time they were thrilled to be there at all?

Storytelling is our task with the next generation, and it starts with loving the story ourselves and telling it as though we believe it—because we believe it. Not every congregation will have a guy like the Urbana storyteller at the lectern or the pulpit, and not every Christian will train in the traditional folk art of storytelling as he and many others are doing. But our young people will only be as passionate about the story as we are ourselves; the rest of the time they simply mirror the blank unconcern they see in the faces of the grown-ups around them. All it took was one gray-haired guy reciting Isaiah to capture the imaginations of twenty thousand youth. What will it take for your congregation?

I believe there are two key storytelling opportunities for the church in youth ministry. The first is corporate worship—not those ancillary "youth worship" times we feel compelled to design in order to "meet their needs," but the *main weekly gathering of the intergenerational faith community*. And the second is catechesis, or intentional discipleship training, sometimes called confirmation. These are the ways we invite the next generation to step into the ongoing story of scripture. This is how we impart the content of faith: its master narrative, language, and culture. Through these storytelling venues, we engage their imaginations, facilitate their formation into the image of Christ, and help them inhabit a narratable world.

Is our worship telling the story in such a way that our young people can't wait to be a part of it week after week? Are we as a congregation living the story in such a way that catechesis—intentional discipleship training—becomes a natural yet vital process of enculturation into the narratable world of the church? These are the questions we'll address in this section.

CHAPTER 6

WORSHIP AS STORY

Our basic struggle, on a Sunday morning, revolves around the questions: Who gets to name the world? Who is authorized to tell the story of what is going on among us?

—WILLIAM WILLIMON

We've already discussed how there's a crisis of story in the worshiping community. But there's also a crisis of story*telling*. Nonliturgical churches have dismissed as irrelevant the narrative arc that has given structure to the church for thousands of years—which means they subsume form under style and replace the voice of the universal church with that of the individual pastor. Meanwhile many liturgical churches have lost sight of what it means to make the story worth telling in the first place. They treat both the text and the liturgy with about the same enthusiasm as the telephone book: the story is no longer enchanting, no longer startling, no longer beloved. And their young people aren't fooled.

Storytelling is an art form; and thankfully, the worshiping church has had more than two thousand years to perfect it. The story isn't the same as the message ("Jesus loves you") or the advertising campaign ("come as you are"), though it certainly can and does encompass those things. The story—like Shakespeare's play—is the Thing itself. It's the life, the world, the experience into which we're inviting our young people. Sure, we may have a series of story-moments or even messages within the worship experience, such as music or drama or the sermon; but the whole thing together is meant to be an inhabitable narrative.

So what does the art of worship-as-story look like?

INGREDIENTS OF NARRATIVE IN WORSHIP

Worship-as-story, like Bible-as-story, contains all the same ingredients as story itself: character, plot, setting, and tone. Without a clear handle on all four ingredients and their importance in narrative, worship tends to become lopsided, emphasizing one ingredient at the expense of the others and eventually degenerating into something other than story. Reclaiming these ingredients is key to storytelling for this generation.

CHARACTER. Who is worship about? This is not an easy question. "Seeker-friendly" churches will tell you it's about the seeker; they focus on meeting the needs of the people coming in the door for the first time. Traditional mainline churches, by contrast, will tell you it's about the members—about meeting the needs of the faithful who constitute the foundational base of the institution. And the debate goes on. Writes one contemporary worship guru, "Various churches across the nation are changing their worship services to meet the needs of the emerging culture."[1] But I can't help wondering: Is worship really about "meeting needs"? Is it about the people at all? Are we, in fact, the main characters in this story?

Worship is about God in Christ.

The answer, I believe, is no. Worship is about God in Christ. I suppose one could argue that if there were no people to do the worshiping, no worship would take place; but scripture paints a different picture. Worship goes on in heaven from the lips of the seraphim (see Isa. 6:2-3), while here on earth—should humans fail to praise—even the stones would cry out (see Luke 19:37-40). Yes, human worshipers play a role, but God is the main protagonist. This story is about Jesus and no other.

So our worship, then, carries the same emphasis as scripture: its goal is to create a "faithful portrait" of God in Christ. Each Sunday the congregation takes out its metaphorical paintbrushes and generates a rendering of his character by telling his story: both the larger story of what God has done for us as a people and the smaller stories of what God is doing in each of our lives. In this way our children and youth come to know the central character, the main protagonist, the axis on which our whole narrative turns.

Given these considerations, I argue there really should be no such thing as "youth worship." We're not trying to paint a "faithful portrait" of youth culture; we're not crafting an experience to "meet the needs" of a certain subset of the population. Youth are not the "who" of worship. Rather, the church should seek to give everyone a voice within the larger worshiping body to tell the story of Jesus from generation to generation. Sure, occasionally youth will worship together within the context of the church's ancillary youth programming (such as, say, at a retreat), just as the adult Bible study will take Communion together, and the women's small groups will spend time in prayer. But this should never eclipse or replace corporate worship, and it most certainly shouldn't focus on "meeting the needs" of that subset of human worshipers. It takes *the entire community*—young, old, male, female, black, white, seekers, and regulars—to paint a truly faithful portrait of our story's central character.

PLOT. As we've already discussed, a story's plot has a beginning, middle, and end consisting of a sequence of events developed around a particular conflict or gradual unveiling. As far as worship-as-story is concerned, this guiding story arc has already been provided for us in the church calendar or liturgical year. It's not a plot we're creating from scratch. Our narrative focuses on the events in the life of Jesus: his birth, life, death, and resurrection. We start with Advent and then move through Christmas, Epiphany, Lent, Holy Week,

Easter, Pentecost, and "Ordinary Time." Within this plotline, each worship service becomes a different chapter in the overall story, with various subplots and sequels woven in.

Sadly, however, plot is where many churches have lost their focus. Thanks to our capitulation to modernism, writes Robert Webber:

> [We've] relegated the Christian concept of time to the list of nonessentials. In the meantime we have baptized the secular calendar. We celebrate the national holidays and Mother's Day while neglecting the story of God's saving action in Advent, Epiphany, Lent, and Pentecost.[2]

We'll talk more about this when we get to the discussion of narrative form, but suffice it to say our weekly worship is not simply a sequence of Sundays; it's a *meaningful* sequence of Sundays. The narrative arc of the church calendar provides a satisfying shape for the God-hungry imagination, giving us a beginning, middle, and end, with all the loose pieces tied together in between. To dismiss this plot is to risk unraveling the story. And if we don't tell this particular plot about our central character, which one do we tell?

Some questions to consider regarding the plot of worship-as-story are these. How does your church's worship throughout the year build from one chapter (or Sunday) of the story to the next while still keeping this particular chapter self-contained? How much backstory are you giving from week to week to allow outsiders to catch up? What sorts of teasers and hints and riddles are you dropping along the way to keep your listeners' interest piqued for next time? And don't forget the magic effect of repetition: just because you've done this before every year doesn't mean it loses its potency (just try changing the plot of a child's favorite bedtime story and see what happens).

As you engage with each chapter or worship service in your church, always keep before you the question, "Where is this whole thing headed, anyway?" Your young people want to know.

SETTING. Thanks to the catchy little hymn, we know the church is not a building; the church is not a steeple; the church is not a dwelling place—the church is a people. Even so, the setting does have a role in the story.[3] Our worship space speaks volumes about our central character and the narrative we claim to be telling. Writes Webber:

> The very narrative of faith which we seek to know and to live is symbolically expressed in our space. We take the ordinary aspects of life—stone, wood, windows, tables, and chairs—and form them into voices of the Christian mystery.[4]

As a young person walks into the building, what story is he or she hearing in wood and stone? Is it of God's grace in the midst of brokenness, of light in the heart of darkness? Or is it about upwardly mobile suburban success, power politics, and material discontent? Is the story being told in a mighty cathedral that speaks of God's glory and majesty, of higher and holier things than school, work, and the mall? Or is it being told in a more contemporary setting that speaks of God's presence in our everyday lives, in our ordinary comings and goings? In what ways do the building and location contribute to the story? In what ways does the setting perhaps detract from the story or tell a different story altogether?

In the midst of these concerns, it's easy to confuse setting with style. One worship leader writes, "Examine your building through the eyes of someone from the emerging culture and decorate accordingly."[5] Rather, I suggest examining your church through the *lens of story*: what story does your worship space tell? If it isn't telling the right story or telling it in the most effective way, consider asking the youth to weigh in on what needs to change.

It's also easy to confuse setting with props. Some worship leaders advocate a return to ancient worship forms, but this seems to entail little more than raiding the church attic to see what sweet props we can find to make our young adult worship feel "vintage." Apparently, "we want students to feel like they are entering *sacred space* when they walk into the room."[6] And yet our students really are entering sacred space, whether they feel like it or not. Even though worship and storytelling are a kind of "play," we must be careful not to use the various physical elements of the setting as if we're merely playing house or making some kind of parody of the ancient story. Our worship space is the house of God; we are indeed God's people; we are living a real story that started before we got here and will continue after we leave.

Also, we must remember that many props and symbols are already freighted with meaning; they're not merely useful this Sunday only to be discarded next week in favor of something else. These things come with stories that preceded us. For example, during one of my first weeks of leading youth group as the new youth director of my church, I found a really cool "Christ candle" in the cupboard. So I thought, *Sweet! We'll use this to create some atmosphere during closing prayer tonight.* But the minute I put it in the center of the group, a chorus of gasps rose from the circle. Without realizing it, I'd lit the candle that a previous youth director had purchased in memory of a student who had died in a car accident. It was a prop that needed very special handling over many weeks and months before it could become a symbol of hope again.

The setting tells a story, along with the physical elements in it. What story is your space telling?

TONE. Tone is the narrative voice or attitude of the storytellers. This goes for everyone, not just the pastor or the worship team but the regulars in the pews as well as the choir, the praise team, the liturgist, the greeters, the sound guys, and the entire seventh-grade confirmation class in the back row. The people live the story; they are the story. If the grown-ups in front and in the pews look bored, no wonder our youth lose interest! And if the youth themselves are falling asleep, no wonder the children crab about being there. As storytellers to the next generation, we must love this story; we must express our passion for it with every fiber of our being, with the very timbre of our voices, with all our verbal and nonverbal behavior.

I remember the first time I found myself among a worshiping community that truly loved the story—that loved telling it in the same way every week, like little kids reading their favorite version of

"Goldilocks and the Three Bears." It was at an Episcopal (now Anglican) church in Chicago's west suburbs that did the full liturgy every Sunday, including the Great Thanksgiving with sung responses. When the white-robed priest looked us in the eyes and *smiled* and said, "Lift up your hearts!" the congregation joyfully responded, "We lift them up to the Lord!" And when he said, "Let us give thanks to the Lord our God!" the people called out, "It is *right* to give our thanks and praise!" And so it went, all the way to the final "amen." Every muscle in their bodies made evident that these people truly believed that *it is indeed a right, and a good and joyful thing*—always and everywhere—to give thanks to the Father Almighty, creator of heaven and earth. They actually *looked* joyful! This was their story, about their beloved God, and they loved telling every word of it. Soon I loved it too, which is what brought me back week after week.

Now, of course, some of that church's enthusiasm was a reflection of the pastor's own demeanor. It goes without saying that the celebrant's attitude has a huge influence on the overall tone or tenor of worship-as-story. The pastor, more than anyone else in the room, plays the role of resident bard in telling the tale: through the Word proclaimed (sermon) and the Word enacted (Eucharist). Says Willimon, "One of the duties of pastors in their preaching is to renarrate our lives in the light of the story of Jesus. Thereby ordinary people have their lives rescripted, caught up in a great drama that is called salvation."[7] In my experience, the best sermons are those that are truly pastoral and possibly even prophetic in tone: they could not have been preached anywhere else to anyone else; and thus their tone tells a story uniquely suited to that particular audience in that particular time.

> *As storytellers to the next generation, we must love this story; we must express our passion for it with every fiber of our being, . . . with all our verbal and nonverbal behavior.*

Unfortunately, it's all too easy for the pastor's narrative voice to eclipse all others, for worshipers to rely so heavily on the leader's tone that it dominates everything else. This is especially true when the other narrative elements—such as plot and character—are dismissed or redefined in favor of cultural relevancy. The only thing left to drive the worship forward is the strength of the pastor's own personality, which means the church risks being drawn into what Webber calls "entertainment worship" rather than true storytelling. The pastor's tone or attitude does matter, but it shouldn't dominate.

What is the tone of your church's worship? How are the people engaged as both hearers and storytellers? What does the expression on their faces say about this story they call the good news? And how are the youth responding?

WORSHIP AND FORM

Permit me, if you will, to climb on a personal soapbox for a moment. We youth workers are notorious for getting hung up on the *style* of our church's worship services—particularly the music, the preaching, and what the guitarist is wearing—and we forget entirely about (or dismiss) the *form*. Let's consider what we've learned so far. Style is merely the cosmetic trappings of a narrative. It's the pastor's tie, the drummer's rhythm, the color of the carpeting in the foyer. Style can and should change. Form, by contrast, is the worship's thematic structure; it's the floor and walls and ceiling of the narrative and how it's put together. Form incarnates the story; it embodies meaning. Without form, style has nothing to hang its fashionable hat on.

Yet too often we let style win the day, creating rifts in the worshiping community that escalate into all-out "worship wars." Writes Webber:

> This conflict of style has continued in the twentieth-century debate about traditional versus contemporary worship. Traditional worship seems to be hanging on to modernity while contemporary worship has capitulated to pop cul-

ture. In either case the debate continues to rage about style with little concern for a biblical theology of worship.[8]

A "biblical theology of worship" is one that structures its narrative around an ancient form or pattern created by the early church. Specifically, that pattern is the fourfold movement of gathering, proclamation, Communion, and sending forth.[9] We see this loosely modeled in Acts 2:42, where we learn that the Pentecost converts "devoted themselves to the apostles' teaching [proclamation] and fellowship [gathering], to the breaking of bread [Communion] and the prayers [sending forth into the world]." In worship-as-story, first we gather the storytellers together in one place; then we tell the story through scripture and preaching; then we live the story in the sacrament of the Eucharist; and finally we turn our focus to a world that needs the story—though not necessarily all in that order. (Notice that music is not mentioned here.)

This fourfold pattern is the narrative form of worship-as-story. It's our basic structure, the floor and walls and ceiling of our narrative. And even though there's tremendous flexibility within that ancient pattern to tell the story of faith in ways that speak to unique cultural contexts, the contemporary church has all but lost sight of this biblical theology of worship in favor of stylistic concerns.

In fact, we call some services "formal" and others "informal" as if it's a matter of personal preference rather than of purpose. Granted, what we tend to mean by "formal" is jackets and ties (back to issues of style again); but theologically speaking, what is really meant is "liturgical." Liturgy is form. The repetitious words, phrases, and scriptural quotations are the *embodiment of story.* Thus liturgy is not a particular style of worship or some outmoded preference on the part of old people; it's a timeless pattern based on the fourfold movement—one that was originally created by first-rate storytellers who knew what they were about. Liturgy embodies the story, which is to say it embodies both the content and the meaning of the Christian faith. It's not a matter of opinion but of function.

So what happens when a worshiping community dismisses liturgy as irrelevant? By now you can probably guess where I'm headed. My contention is that in losing the liturgy, the worshiping community risks losing its narrative shape—which means, if all we've learned about form so far is true, the community risks losing both the story itself and its *meaning*. The church no longer inhabits a narratable world.

Unfortunately, the very churches that are best situated to reclaim liturgical form as vital to worship-as-story are the churches that are dismissing it altogether. Here I think of the recent seminary graduate who was about to be appointed to a United Methodist church where the pastor proudly confided that he had "gutted the liturgy" in the face of much opposition from what he called "neo-Catholics" in the congregation. The graduate wisely bowed out and went somewhere else. He recognized that if you've gutted the liturgy, you've slaughtered the story; so why stick around for what's left, especially when it's nothing more than the personality-driven stand-up routine of the pastor?

That church isn't an isolated case. Many mainline and traditionally liturgical churches are "gutting" the liturgy, and they seem to be doing this for one of two reasons. On the one hand, they want to be "successful" like the seeker-friendly, nondenominational, informal churches down the road (and I can't help asking, from a storytelling standpoint, successful in what way?). On the other hand, they wish to discard the old liturgical language as being too conservative in favor of new, more "inclusive" language—which, unhappily, more often speaks about their theological bias than about the ongoing story. I recently heard a pastor invite us to listen "for" the Word of God instead of "to" the Word of God. I was struck by the difference a few letters make. Listening "for" puts the onus on us to cobble together meaning out of a stream of otherwise random verbiage, whereas listening "to" puts the onus on the Word to be the Word whether we get it (or like it) or not. Even the tiniest prepositions speak volumes about what we think of this story we're telling.

So I wonder: What if those churches that come out of a more liturgical heritage were to dive even deeper into that heritage rather than continually watering it down or excising the "offensive" parts till there's nothing even remotely interesting about the liturgy anymore? What if the church joyfully kept the form as a beloved story rather than as a matter of personal taste—and along the way remembered to explain it to new generations rather than assuming everyone out there understood what was going on and what it meant?

And my concern isn't only about traditionally liturgical communities. To those of us who pride ourselves on being "informal," I'd encourage us to consider what story we could possibly be telling without form. Is our story merely about how cool our pastor is and how loud our subwoofers are? Or have we truly developed a biblical theology of worship that imparts the only story that really matters to the next generation?

Finally, to my youth ministry colleagues I offer still another challenge. What if we put form over style for once and got down to the real business of storytelling again?

I don't say this lightly. If we as a church are truly concerned about "pervasive teen inarticulacy" when it comes to the biblical and theological content of faith, then we need look no further than what happens in worship on a Sunday morning. This isn't a situation in which "anything goes" based on the pastor's or the people's personal tastes. Reclaiming the story means reclaiming the form as our basic structure, whether this follows the classic liturgy of the ancient church or a very intentional yet faithful recrafting flavored by the context we find ourselves in. And if at any point we wonder whether form really "works" in helping young adults inhabit a narratable world, perhaps we should pay attention to their unexpected migrations toward such things as high Anglicanism, Orthodoxy, Catholicism, Taizé, house churches, and the "new monasticism"—all of which seek to embody and express the story of Jesus in decidedly liturgical, as well as countercultural, ways.[10]

Call me a neo-Catholic if you like, but I posit that the current hunger for liturgy is due in part to an awareness that we live in a world that has lost its story—a world that desperately needs story. And it's also due to an awareness that the storyteller is not just the pastor, who otherwise sets the tone according to his or her own personality and preferences. The storyteller is the *whole* church—past, present, and future. The hunger for liturgy is more than merely incidental or even trendy. It's a cry from the God-hungry imagination. It reflects a growing awareness that the language and culture of the historic church do indeed matter if the church of today is to be the living story that began before we got here and will continue long after we're gone.

CLOSING THOUGHTS: HOW WORSHIP-AS-STORY WORKS

I close with some thoughts on how worship-as-story works in nurturing the God-hungry imagination of our young people. The example comes to mind of the little boy at our church who came forward for the children's sermon one Sunday in Advent. Up front was the Jesse Tree, a bare set of branches to which new ornaments were added each week that told the story of Jesus' ancestry. The tree was loaded down with stars, tent, staff, coat of many colors, crown, and so forth, and the children added even more ornaments while they helped the pastor retell the story. But then it came time for them to leave the sanctuary for children's church. As the little boy was being carried out by his father, he wailed, "But I want to stay with the Judy Tree! I want to stay!"

Worship-as-story isn't or shouldn't be a purely passive experience. It invites us to step inside something larger than ourselves.

Of course the middle schoolers in my Sunday school class later recounted this with much hilarity, even as they admitted that the Jesse Tree—now affectionately known as Judy—was pretty cool. Sure, they no longer went up front for children's time during worship; but they were listening.

When well told and well lived by the storytellers, worship, like story itself, offers opportunities for the imagination to be nurtured and transformed. It offers the chance for engagement, meaningful synthesis, vision, empathy, and creative response—in fact, the various movements within our fourfold pattern are suited for just those opportunities: (1) we engage with one another as we gather; (2) we synthesize what we hear in the reading and proclamation of the Word—while catching a vision for our own part in the story; (3) we empathize with the sufferings of Christ in the Eucharist; and (4) this sends us forth in creative response to a hurting world. The fourfold pattern provides a memorable shape for the imagination and, through the power of the Holy Spirit, helps us make meaningful connections between the church, the world, and our lives.

Worship-as-story isn't or shouldn't be a purely passive experience. It invites us to step inside something larger than ourselves; and thus, like story itself, worship *works*: it offers experiences of transcendence and timelessness, resonance and wonder, intimacy and identity, mystery and enchantment. As grown-ups, for whom worship has become mere routine, we tend to forget such responses are possible. But for children and even youth, the story can be compelling, especially if they're personally invited to help tell it.

Let's not forget that our young people, when experiencing a story, require very little by way of technological embellishment or even style, as long as the grown-up storytellers are fully engaged and the story is worth hearing. When it comes to youth ministry specifically, let's not dismiss the essential form or *substance* of worship in favor of the style or *toppings*; otherwise we starve the God-hungry imaginations of our young people—many of whom really do want to stay for a story that matters.

QUESTIONS AND EXERCISES

1. Consider the ingredients of narrative in your church's main worship service (character, plot, setting, tone). Who is your worship about? What is the plot of the story from beginning to end? How does your setting contribute to or detract from the story? What's the overall tone (e.g., are people glad to be there?), and who sets the tone? In short, what story is your worship service telling?

2. When it comes to the narrative form or structure of your church's worship service, what aspects of the ancient church's fourfold pattern are strongest: gathering, proclamation, communion, or sending forth? Which ones are weakest? Why?

3. In your church's approach to worship with youth, how easy is it to emphasize style over form? How might you encourage your students, their leaders, and parents to reclaim a biblical theology of worship?

IDEA FOR THE ROAD

Take your students to worship at a church that comes from a different tradition than yours. Afterwards discuss their reactions based on the questions raised in numbers 1 and 2 above. From their perspective, what story is that church telling?

FARE FOR THE IMAGINATION

Adolescents are looking for a soul-shaking, heart-waking, world-changing God to fall in love with; and if they do not find that God in the Christian church, they will most certainly settle for lesser gods elsewhere.

—KENDA CREASY DEAN AND RON FOSTER[11]

CHAPTER 7

THE ART OF IMMERSION

Catechesis means impressing upon youth a
Life, not a religion.
—KENDA DEAN AND RON FOSTER

t this point in our discussion, it's easy to feel a bit discouraged. After all, not many of us youth workers are in the position to heavily influence what happens in the main worship service of the congregation we serve. We can't single-handedly silence the competing narratives in the pews; we can't strong-arm the leadership into focusing on form over style; we can't make the people love this story they're telling. Sometimes the most we can do is become conscientious objectors in the stylistic worship wars while gently reminding the leadership (and the youth themselves) that this story is not ultimately about any of us. Then when we do have the chance to shape a worship experience, we can model a biblical theology of worship that invites everyone—including youth—to inhabit a narratable world.

In the meantime, another opportunity often gets dumped in our laps, and that's the church's confirmation program, or catechesis. Generally speaking, confirmation is the one youth program that will happen (in the mainline church), whether or not there's a hired youth staff person to lead it. And even when there is a hired youth worker, the senior pastor isn't always willing to change how confirmation happens. But more often than not, the leadership is happy to cede programmatic control to us, at which point confirmation should be more than just an annoying blip on our ministerial radar. I've come to believe that confirmation is one of the most important and serendipitous storytelling opportunities we in youth ministry will ever have. This chapter explores some of my thoughts on how this might happen effectively.

But before we dive in, I offer a word to those who serve in churches without a tradition of catechetical training. Before you dismiss this chapter as possibly irrelevant to your context, I invite you to consider how it might be helpful for discipleship in general, whether in small-group ministries or student leadership or any other area of intentional training. How are your young people learning about and practicing the language and culture of your worshiping community?

THE TASK OF CATECHESIS

Catechesis is an ancient form of intensive instruction that prepares a candidate (also known as the *catechumen,* or "hearer") for baptism. In the past few centuries, it has come to include those who were baptized as infants: their intentional spiritual nurture continues as they grow old enough to understand and confirm who they are in Christ. This is, in part, what the church means by *confirmation.*

Many of our forebears were taught to approach confirmation from a purely cerebral standpoint. To borrow language from postliberal theologian George Lindbeck,[1] the modern church tended to take the "cognitive-propositional" approach, which says in essence, "Here are the basic facts you need to know about the universe; here's the logical format of our belief system. To be a Christian is to accept this set of a priori statements." The content of confirmation consisted of little more than memorizing the Nicene Creed or the Westminster Shorter Catechism without any attempt to link those "admirably compact form[s] of storytelling" with the individual lives of the catechumens sitting in the pews.

At the other end of the spectrum is what Lindbeck calls the "experiential-expressive" (or emotion-based) approach, which says in essence, "Remember that feeling you got when you helped the homeless guy? That's genuine spirituality. Christians merely use Christian terminology to express their a priori spiritual experience." This experiential approach is the dominant attitude toward religion in today's culture, particularly among Baby Boomers who were soured by their mind-numbingly boring confirmation training as teenagers in mainline or Roman Catholic churches. They didn't see their elders walking (or even emoting) the talk, so they figured the talk was meaningless unless you felt something first. And this may be true to a certain extent, but how does this make Christian spirituality any different from, say, Buddhism?

So all along, the modern church has pushed the cognitive-propositional approach even as postmodern teens (and their parents) have pushed back against whatever doesn't sync with their experiential-expressive impulses—and needless to say, the results have not been happy or fruitful. Which means if we're going to get anywhere in the discipleship training of our young, the church would do well to embrace the third alternative that Lindbeck proposes, the "cultural-linguistic" approach. This says, "Being a Christian requires embracing the 'alien Christian language and form of life,'[2] so here's how to become fluent in it yourself." In other words, it's about *enculturation*: the gradual process of becoming a fully fluent member of a foreign society by immersion in its way of life.

The more I consider the "cultural-linguistic" approach, the more I'm convinced it's not merely a helpful way of looking at the catechetical process; it *is* the catechetical process. From ancient times discipleship training has involved learning the biblical narrative and theological language of the Christian community: this is the content of catechesis. But it's also about the learner's willing reception of that content and her determination to practice and live by it, as I've stated before. It's about her embracing the *whole culture* of the worshiping community in which the content is experienced and lived. In fact, the confirmand must be willing to give up her previous culture for the new—and by *previous* I don't mean secular pop culture but rather Moralistic Therapeutic Deism, that me-centered and amorphous substitute for historic Christianity. Like Nicodemus the Pharisee, she's giving up whatever she thought religion was for the true kingdom.

Unfortunately, church leadership too often capitulates to youthful and parental pressure that would make confirmation as fluffy, fun, and noncommittal as possible. If intentional teaching happens at all, it happens in vague terms that bring it "down to their level" without bringing it back up again to the level of biblical orthodoxy. Write Kenda Dean and Ron Foster: "Because we hope youth will chart their own course (to a degree, often, that would never occur to us were the subject algebra instead of religion), we allude to faith more often than we proclaim it."[3] The experiential-expressive approach wins out even over cognitive-propositional concerns, and thus enculturation by full immersion doesn't even register on the list of possibilities.

But when a confirmand stands up in front of our congregation on Confirmation Sunday, we're not asking her to talk about what God means to her. Nor are we asking her to acknowledge a set of propositional statements about the universe. Rather, we're inviting her to step inside an ongoing story and become one of its characters for the rest of her life. It's less like a math test and more like a game of jump rope: it's not about passing or failing or even emoting but about watching, practicing, and jumping in.

TEACHING THE CULTURE

Classical Christianity did this enculturation as preparation for baptism.[4] While the candidate was becoming familiar with the stories and language of the people through one-on-one mentoring and small-group instruction, she was simultaneously immersed in the culture of the worshiping community. So even in the midst of her linguistic and narrative training, the community's rituals, practices, symbols, beliefs, values, habits, and customs were being demonstrated and reinforced through the behavior and attitudes of the people. The catechumen may even have adopted these behaviors and attitudes before she fully understood their biblical or theological significance. Then, after a sufficient time of study and enculturation (three years, in fact), the student was baptized. Afterwards she was invited to the table to partake of Communion for the first time. She was now a member of the priesthood of all believers, a full citizen in the kingdom of God.

When it comes to catechesis or confirmation today (whether in preparation for baptism or reaffirmation of it), I believe that learning the culture of the worshiping community still requires full immersion in that community's way of life for a significant period of time. And I'm not talking about just showing up once a week for several months or years, vital as weekly worship and teaching are to ongoing spiritual formation. I'm talking about a series of formative events leading up to a week or more of full participation in the daily life and practices of the people, from the moment a young person wakes up in the morning to when she drops into bed at night.

I'm talking about *camp*.

Sometime during my second year in full-time youth ministry, our church went along with my crazy idea to do confirmation as a series of retreats leading up to a full week of summer camp. I'd served for one summer at a nondenominational camp ministry, so I'd seen what happens to kids when they're fully immersed in a Christian community long enough to learn the routine and the lingo. It's amazing what one week can accomplish. It's even more amazing what one week can do within the context of your home church, alongside people you've known for much of your life, who will be there to support you afterwards.

We started by finding a recreational lodge not too far from our town that could host eight to twelve students and their leaders, with occasional guests popping in for meals and other events. So we were close enough to home that mentors and parents could staff the camp, but not so close that it felt like the "same old, same old" life our kids had always known. Then I structured the camp schedule around a daily rhythm of Christian practice, study, and play, with the teaching sessions following the basic biblical narrative from old to new covenant. We started each day after breakfast with "Holy

Ground" time, during which the students spent twenty minutes alone, reading and meditating on our key scriptures for the day. Then we went into our first teaching session, followed by an ongoing craft project led by a member of the congregation. After lunch we generally had another teaching session, followed by free time before dinner; and we closed the day with worship, which the students were planning and leading by the end of the week.

Throughout the week we sprinkled a variety of field trips, including canoeing on a nearby river, a colossal game of Capture the Flag, a visit to a historic Native American United Methodist church, and a service project at the local food pantry, among other group-building and formative activities. Our pastor and other leaders joined us for teaching sessions and evening worship while church members stopped in daily to lead craft projects, drop off snacks, slip notes into the students' mailboxes, and join us for meals. On the last night during the evening Communion service, we surprised the students with letters from their parents that expressed the parents' hopes, prayers, and blessings for their child.

When I look back on my seven years in full-time ministry, confirmation camp was the most formative experience I had the privilege to facilitate in the lives of those kids. Sure, the retreats that led up to it were good for group building, and other activities throughout the year helped them build relationships with their mentors and other key adults. But camp was when they stepped into the story. That's when all the loose ends of their otherwise disconnected lives began to be woven into a comprehensible pattern that nurtured their imaginations—without continual sabotage from the outside world. That's when the alien culture of the worshiping community they took part in on Sundays suddenly began to feel like home. They were no longer strangers in a strange land. They were a people.

Confirmation camp still continues in that congregation every summer, though I'm no longer the resident bard. That's because the whole church, not just the pastor or youth leader, has become the storyteller. They recognize that to be fully immersed in the baptismal waters of the Christian faith takes the entire pool of the worshiping community.

Meanwhile, without realizing it, our church adopted a formative pattern that several theological schools around the country are now offering for older youth. I've had the privilege to participate in one through the Duke Youth Academy for Christian Formation at Duke Divinity School.[5] And I was delighted to discover that our two weeks were based on the same kind of rhythm of Christian practice, study, service, and play that our church had intuitively crafted for its youth. Except this time the students were rising juniors and seniors from all over the country, representing dozens of denominations; and our resident bards were world-renowned theologians and scholars who used really, really big words. But guess what? The students were speaking those words before the end of the two weeks. And that's because they were fully immersed in a worshiping community that reinforced the normative language and culture until the students themselves were fluent in it.

Granted, not every church can offer its confirmands a week or more of camp; and not every church can send its high school students to a theological school for part of the summer. But every church can treat each discipleship class and each worship service as an opportunity for continual rehearsal of what the words, stories, symbols, rituals, and experiences in the Christian community mean. Here I think of my husband's seminary classmate who was placed at a vibrant Anglican church for his summer field education.[6] Two or three times a year, the leadership takes the congregation through the liturgy by explaining each part of it and what it means. In addition, the church regularly posts a blurb in the bulletin and on its Web site that says,

Every church can treat each discipleship class and each worship service as an opportunity for continual rehearsal of what the words, stories, symbols, rituals, and experiences in the Christian community mean.

"Did you know?" regarding some liturgical practice or symbol. And meanwhile the "toys" in children's church are the props of *Godly Play*,[7] so they're all connected to Bible stories, the liturgical year, worship, and the sacraments.

If the imagination is the "organ of meaning" that helps us put things together, then the formative nature of our discipleship process is precisely this task of making cultural-linguistic connections. From day to day and week to week, we weave together the loose ends of our students' lives, helping them connect word and image, story and practice, school and home, church and everything else. We nurture their imaginations so they can fully engage in the worshiping community—not as foreigners, but as fully fluent fellow citizens.

TEACHING THE THEOLOGICAL LANGUAGE

"Religious language," write the authors of *Soul Searching*, "is like any other language: to learn how to speak it, one needs first to listen to native speakers using it a lot, and then one needs plenty of practice at speaking it oneself."[8] If the church is to address the current crisis of "pervasive teen inarticulacy" when it comes to faith, we must intentionally teach the theological language we use to talk about it. We must unapologetically tell our youth and catechumens, "Yes, we speak Christianese around here; and you're gonna learn it."

In the specialized sphere of academia, theology consists of the shorthand terminology theologians use to communicate with other theologians—for example, *soteriology*, is one's understanding of salvation. In the context of the local church, meanwhile, theology is the shorthand Christians use to communicate with other Christians—for example, *grace*, or God's free gift of salvation. The Christian community first came up with theological abstractions because eventually we had to speak in shorthand about the complexity of God's story and character, or we'd never get anywhere in regular discourse with one another.

Often a community's theological heritage can be known by the kinds of abstractions it employs—for example, *prevenient grace* is the work of the Holy Spirit in one's life before one is aware, as understood in Methodism. That's why a large part of the church's task in the training of its youth is teaching the theological language of both the historical and the local church. Not only must we teach the language, but more importantly we must use it ourselves—and use it a lot. And we must encourage and provide opportunities for youth to use it too.

Again, I'll refer to my experience at Duke Youth Academy as an example. Our director, Fred Edie, assistant professor of Christian Education at the divinity school, had us wrap up each morning plenary session by singing a new stanza of "He's Got the Whole World in His Hands" using language we'd just learned. So on the day we learned about covenant, we sang, "He's got the covenantal community in his hands, he's got the covenantal community . . ." And, of course, Fred had us clapping along and singing at the top of our lungs, which lent the whole experience a kind of tongue-twisting hilarity that made it both fun and unforgettable. How's that for teaching theological language and putting it to immediate use!

It's pretty exciting when youth start using the lingo they've heard during their time with us. And certainly a good test of how much content they're actually absorbing is their fluency in the shorthand we use to talk about it. But a word of caution on this point. We seem to think that the more we can train teenagers to express faith through abstract statements, the more they comprehend it. If, for example, they can correctly answer the questions from the Westminster Shorter Catechism, we suppose we're getting somewhere; we've done our job. But is that really the case? Is teaching the theological abstractions the end of the catechetical road?

If all we've learned about the imagination and story is true, we should aim for one last important step. After we've helped youth achieve some fluency in theological abstractions, we should then be training them to think as *concretely* as possible again—specifically, to be able to express themselves effectively in metaphor to those who don't understand the abstractions. We want the analogical ability of their imagination fully operative so they can articulate "what God is like." Metaphor (meaning "to carry across") is how they bridge two cultures, two languages, two communities; it's how they express the culture of Christianity to those who don't know it. Otherwise, if all they're left with is abstractions, they'll never leave the Christian cloister where everyone talks just like them. To leave the cloister is to enter the world of the concrete again, to enter the realm of metaphor.

Religion itself deals in what literary types call "root metaphors": life is like a journey, an adventure, a tree branching up and out. Your faith system determines which metaphors define your life and sense of purpose. The difference with the Christian use of metaphor, however, is that we're not being merely subjective when we speak of what God is like. Our expressions must plumb with both scripture and orthodox Christian belief. So, for example, we can get away with saying God is like a mother comforting a child (Isa. 66:13), but most likely we will not get away with saying God is like a many-breasted fertility goddess. Not all metaphors are created equal.

> *Religion itself deals in what literary types call "root metaphors."*

Meanwhile, we also recognize the natural limits of metaphor as a form. We can only take an analogy so far before it begins to break down. Metaphor theory tells us that all of language is littered with dead metaphors, otherwise known as clichés. These are phrases that have lost their potency—except perhaps to children and nonnative speakers. I remember that while I was an exchange student in East Africa I told my Kenyan roommate, "Don't believe that guy; he's just pulling your leg." The look on her face was worth the airfare there and back. All of a sudden, what had been a dead metaphor for me came alive and starting kicking. I had no idea what to do with it. Like a joke, a living metaphor loses all vitality if it must be taken apart and painstakingly explained. Eventually I gave up.

"Like fish, when metaphors get old, they go bad," writes Christian poet Jeanne Murray Walker,[9] and nowhere is that more apparent than among Christians on a Sunday morning. Not only is our discourse littered with religious clichés ("I once was lost, but now am found"), but we mix our metaphors to a degree that astounds the uninitiated, who tend to take things at face value. "I was blind," says an old-time revivalist during the sharing of joys and concerns, "but then I was washed in the blood of the Lamb, and now I'm found." And while the pastor then blithely moves on to the prayers of the people, the poor fifth grader in the back row is still trying to figure out what bad vision and being washed in blood have to do with each other. Gross.

Some people's imaginations seemed wired for metaphors more so than others. You notice this in confirmation class, no doubt. An analogy that works for one student may not work for another, and no amount of explaining will help the clueless person "get it." There are also some youth who bring very few nuances to the metaphors or analogies they do comprehend on some level. They seem unable to juggle more than one layer of meaning at a time. Meanwhile, others are able to peel back layer after layer, even as they recognize the limitations of metaphor to hold up indefinitely under that kind of scrutiny. We must take all of these differences into account as we assess the analogical ability of the students in our charge.

Middle schoolers have just stepped onto the bridge between the concrete and the abstract, which means they're just beginning to parse the intended meaning of metaphor from its literal sense. So to them, analogical devices become a new kind of game for seeing how many levels of meaning a bald statement might in fact have, as witnessed by their increasing interest in and employment of sexual innuendo. Such things have been known to sabotage even the best of confirmation lessons. The trick is steering this new interest in wordplay into genuine biblical and theological engagement.

Meanwhile, high schoolers approach metaphor with eye-rolling boredom. They've heard it all before. Everything sounds clichéd from overuse. So these older students are ready to be startled by new, strange, jarring, and unlikely metaphors. And they're also ready for the challenge of coming up with new metaphors that express faith within their unique context. We should encourage them in this quest even as we challenge them to use the theological shorthand they've been taught.

After all, we applaud students for employing metaphor when they're in creative writing class because it means clearness and potency of expression. A writer who can deal well with metaphors not only comprehends her material but is able to help others comprehend it too. Abstract expressions and clichés are just plain bad writing. In other words, they're what we use when we're either too lazy to come up with a better expression or we're in a hurry. Writes C. S. Lewis:

> To speak more plainly, he who would increase the meaning and decrease the meaningless verbiage in his own speech and writing, must do two things. He must become conscious of the fossilized metaphors in his words; and he must freely use new metaphors, which he creates for himself.[11]

This isn't to say we don't continue to teach our students the abstract theological shorthand or encourage them to use it. But rather we train youth to use metaphor when expressing themselves to those outside the circle of faith—not through dead metaphors or clichés, nor by casually mixing metaphors, but with very careful attention to what they're saying. And we especially encourage them to craft new metaphors that provide bridges for their hearers from one world to another.

Crafting new metaphors is exactly what Tolkien and Lewis were doing with their fantasy stories, Lewis in particular. This is how he was able to strip the well-worn Christian story of its "stained-glass and Sunday school associations" and "steal past those watchful dragons" of his hearers' usual defenses. Flannery O'Connor, the famous Southern short-story writer, was attempting the same thing. She wrote, "To the hard of hearing you shout, and for the almost-blind you draw large and startling figures."[12] Through her stories she drew "large and startling figures" that recast things like baptism in a shockingly violent light (after all, through baptism we *die* to sin). And there are contemporary Christians doing similar things through film and the arts. How can we encourage young people—particularly our older high school and college students—to create new metaphors for their own generation?

One of the ways we help youth develop this metaphoric ability is by involving them in planning worship. I saw this both at confirmation camp and at Duke Youth Academy. When the students had the stuff of storytelling in their hands—when they were charged with engaging the imaginations of their hearers through worship-as-story—they were forced to shed the abstract theological lingo as well as the dead metaphors of their regular religious verbiage and find new and often surprising ways of communicating.

Sometimes the result was beautiful, poignant, or even poetic. Other times it was downright hilarious. I recall the confirmation group that decided their "message" for worship would be a skit based on the final scenes from *Indiana Jones and the Last Crusade*. As Indy arrived in the chamber where he must try to guess which chalice was the true cup of Christ, the assortment of vessels and glasses were whatever the kids could find around camp, including a crumpled paper cup. So the twelve-year-old Indy looked them over, muttering to himself in his best Harrison Ford impression, and suddenly I realized he was saying, "Jesus was the son of a cardboard salesman . . . Jesus was the son of a cardboard salesman . . ." And so, of course, he picked the *paper* cup, without cracking a smile, as the rest of us roared with laughter.

He chose wisely.

CLOSING THOUGHTS

Youth are natural-born storytellers. Our task in discipleship training is to steer them into a particular storytelling tradition—that is, the narrative, language, and culture of the Christian faith as it has been lived and expressed for two thousand years. This isn't to sideline other concerns, namely that they be "doers of the Word" and not merely hearers. But even more importantly we're training them to live the story. Articulation is one thing; living a certain way because you believe your own words is another. Youth are storytellers by virtue of the story their lives are telling—when their friends are watching, and when they are not.

My emphasis on training youth to be articulate storytellers is born out of this book's primary concern that mainstream American young people are highly inarticulate about the faith they supposedly claim. And yet these same young people, according to *Soul Searching*, seem perfectly able to articulate other subjects, such as sex education or the dangers of substance abuse.[13] Until an otherwise coherent young person can express even the simplest language of faith (e.g., "I believe in Jesus Christ"), we quite rightly must address the church's failure to impart its basic biblical and theological content. And we do so by reclaiming a cultural-linguistic model of catechesis that immerses a young person in the narrative and language of the worshiping community until she is fluent enough to share it with others.

One final thought before I close this section. In the past few years I've begun to wonder if all aspects of youth ministry—retreats, mission trips, youth group, Sunday school, small groups, mentoring, special events—shouldn't be woven in some way into the overall catechetical process, either leading up to confirmation or spinning off of it. Again, it's about making connections, feeding the God-hungry imagination, helping our youth inhabit a narratable world.

QUESTIONS AND EXERCISES

1. How is youth discipleship (confirmation or catechesis) generally perceived by your congregation? by the youth? the parents? the pastor? by you?

2. What might the "cultural-linguistic" model for confirmation look like in your context? What are some ways you can more fully immerse your confirmands in the language and culture of the worshiping community?

3. How can you engage your students as storytellers? In what ways can they be creating new metaphors for communicating the faith to their peers?

IDEA FOR THE ROAD

With your team of youth leaders, make a list of all the cultural differences a person experiences when he or she visits a foreign country (e.g.: language, dress, customs, food, etc.). Then discuss:

- In what ways is our church like a little culture of its own?
- How are we helping our confirmands become proficient in our language and way of life?

FARE FOR THE IMAGINATION

To become religious involves becoming skilled in the language, the symbol system of a given religion. To become a Christian involves learning the story of Israel and of Jesus well enough to interpret and experience oneself and one's world in its terms.

—GEORGE LINDBECK[14]

PART 5

PRACTICAL CONCERNS

We draw people to Christ not by loudly discrediting what they believe, by telling them how wrong they are and how right we are, but by showing them a light that is so lovely that they want with all their hearts to know the source of it.

—MADELEINE L'ENGLE

Tell me a story," a college friend of mine used to say whenever we found ourselves at the same table in the dining hall. This was our moment of youthful rebellion. While everyone around us gobbled up their meals in a frantic rush to the next class or the next social obligation, we obstinately sat and listened to another human being—something that can't be done in a hurry. We sought that brief moment of sanity which comes with the words "Once upon a time," that deep sigh of satisfaction with the words "the end." We sought those experiences only story can provide, experiences that our crazy college days could never give us: timelessness, transcendence, intimacy, identity, mystery, subversion, enchantment, wonder, play, resonance, world building. We sought each other's stories because we needed to remember the Great Story, the one that began long before we got there and would continue long after we left—long after our classes were over and the dining hall crumbled to dust and our names were etched on gravestones in different parts of the world.

"Tell me a story." Last fall I was at a university soccer game with a fellow English-major-turned-youth-worker who was in the midst of completing her final semester of divinity school. Like me, she'd had a wonderfully creative and dreamy childhood, full of long afternoons surrounded by good books. Also like me, her undergraduate major in English had only deepened her love for stories. But now she sat there in the bleachers, after three years of seminary, grieving the loss of a world she once knew: the playful, creative, dreaming, poetic, story-building world, a world that her theological education—for all its emphasis on "right thinking" and "right doing" but rarely "right dreaming"—had all but destroyed.

"Tell me a story," says the poem by Robert Penn Warren. "In this century, and moment, of mania . . . Tell me a story of deep delight." It's a request I'm convinced we Christians should make more often. We should make this request of our pastors, our seminary professors, our parents, our friends, lest the light in our imaginations dim to a mere flicker and the world grow dark around us. Because if there is no light by which we see, no Great Story that illumines our days—and no Storyteller—then we have no source by which to enchant the young people in our charge.

—✺—

This section is for those of us involved in church youth ministry in one form or another. It's about our role as bards and storytellers. In the midst of the church's regularly scheduled programming, we youth workers naturally find ourselves in the position of articulating the story of scripture through teaching and worship. And we find ourselves sharing smaller stories, personal testimonies or excerpts from great literature and film, as a way to build relationships and sneak past our hearers' usual defenses. Often we'll embody key theological themes within metaphors or illustrations we've picked up from various sources, for better or worse. Storytelling, we tend to think, is one of those indispensable tools youth workers keep in their box of tricks, along with Chubby Bunny and Capture the Flag.

But however we engage in narrative, we must always remember that story and metaphor are not merely superfluous embellishments meant to decorate the truth so it's easier to swallow. Story isn't ancillary to what we're really trying to say. Rather, it *embodies* what we're trying to say. It incarnates meaning, gives form to content. We don't treat it as merely an illustration of our main point. Instead (particularly with scripture and worship) the story *is* the point.

As I've already said, rather than trying to be stand-up comedians seeking to entertain or lecturers seeking to inform, we should become bards seeking to enchant. We are poets, "speech-weavers," who thread together the many loose ends of our students' lives by helping them make narrative connections between scripture, school, church, friendships, work, leisure, and home. Throughout the programmatic year we intentionally create "story-moments" that connect everything in the youth ministry back to the Master Story of scripture as lived out in the worshiping community.

So how do we go about this task? Well, here are some miscellaneous thoughts I've been mulling over, based on my own experience and the various conversations taking place in youth ministry today.

CHAPTER 8

THE YOUTH PASTOR AS BARD

*My story is this: I've fallen in love again with
the hero of the story, and I'll never be the same.
Sometimes though, I must confess, I still love
the storytelling more than I love the story itself.*

—JIMMY DAVIS

BARDS VERSUS EVANGELISTS?

The emerging church places heavy emphasis on the "missional" approach to ministry, in which outreach to and evangelization of postmodern culture is the goal. This approach is rightly based on the ministry methods of Paul, with the biblical account of Acts 17 (Paul's speech to the Athenians on Mars Hill) as the seminal example. It insists that postmoderns are a generation of sophisticated pagans who are spiritually seeking, whose postmodern culture is quite foreign from church culture—which means the church must reinvent itself if it's going to be "culturally relevant." In this model the youth pastor is missionary to a foreign culture for whom the gospel is entirely new; he or she is a Christian among sophisticated pagans who are curious and interested, as in Acts 17. Here the emphasis is on the *message*.

Intercultural ministry is a worthy endeavor and one very dear to my heart—in fact, it was the emphasis of my undergraduate major in Christian education. The missional mind-set is indispensable when working with media-saturated and/or unchurched teens, as I've experienced firsthand. But I'm not always certain that the churched teenagers we work with are an alien culture of pagan seekers so much as they are younger versions of their parents, content to play it spiritually safe. If that means going along with Mom when she says church isn't optional, then so be it. This syncs with the findings of *Soul Searching*, which indicate that today's young people are in fact quite conventional and see themselves as religious rather than spiritually seeking,[1] even though their "religion" unconsciously bears little resemblance to the historical and creedal beliefs of Christian orthodoxy. In this respect, according to *Soul Searching*, they look more like their parents than anything else, which means they're not as alien as we've been taught to think.

> *As youth workers, we more often find ourselves in the position of Jesus on the lakeshore than of Paul at Mars Hill.*

It also means that as youth workers, we more often find ourselves in the position of Jesus on the lakeshore than of Paul at Mars Hill: we face a mixed crowd of bored, apathetic, quasi-believers who think they've heard it all rather than a completely foreign culture of sophisticated pagans who are spiritually seeking. We find we must take the bardic-parabolic approach rather than the missional-evangelistic approach, which means we hand-select a small group of disciples who are ready to give up everything to follow the savior—to *those* we reveal "the secrets of the kingdom" through enculturation in the catechetical basics of the faith—while to the rest, to the gathered crowd, we tell stories. If the crowd is annoyed and frustrated because it's not paintball and they don't "get it," oh well. If, after marinating in the metaphors of our parables, they're challenged to see God and the kingdom in a new way, so much the better. Whatever the case, we leave the results to the Holy Spirit.

The youth-pastor-as-bard is charged with expressing the language, narrative, and culture of the kingdom to listeners who think they already know what the kingdom is all about. For the leader among quasi-believers who are bored and mostly apathetic, who think they know all about "God and stuff," the emphasis is on *story*.

This shift in paradigm doesn't mean we dispense with the youth-pastor-as-missionary model, however. Indeed, Jesus regularly interacted with other cultures, including the Samaritan woman and various Roman leaders. Rather, I propose we approach youth ministry with two models rather than one. Yes, we include the missional-evangelistic model of Paul as appropriate and necessary when working with unchurched youth who seem captured and defined by popular culture. But we must also include the bardic-parabolic model of Jesus as vital to our work with those teens who've been raised in some version of the faith—which, according to *Soul Searching*, is a larger majority than we've been led to think.

The youth-pastor-as-bard takes a different approach from the missionary-evangelist, though both are essentially about the same thing. The evangelist spells out the truth in language the hearer can understand. The storyteller, by contrast, subverts the meaning in language the hearer will listen to but may not understand immediately. The missionary takes the burden of being understood upon himself by learning the language and the culture; the storyteller leaves the hearer's understanding up to the Holy Spirit. So the hearer didn't get it (yet)? Oh well: on to the next story and the next audience.

Certainly, as so many youth ministry leaders insist, we must have a good handle on the language our hearers speak and the language we ourselves use. But for the missional youth pastor, it's about the language of the *story*; for the youth-pastor-as-bard, it's about the language of the story. To use C. S. Lewis's distinction, perhaps we could even say that for the evangelistic youth minister, it's about *truth*; for the bardic youth minister, it's about *meaning*. Both approaches are necessary and appropriate. But they are different and depend on the context.

As Christian teachers and preachers (may I once again reiterate), we must always remember that we're not meant to be journalists, merely relaying the facts; we're meant to be bards, speech-weavers, spinning a spell that captures the imagination. Yes, the gospel is the "good news" like a front-page headline about a landmark treaty between warring parties; but, as we've already discussed, the gospel is just as importantly the "good spell," a Word that has the power to capture and transform the human imagination.

One final thought on this issue: in the church today we face the enormous challenge of working with youth who are not consistently present from week to week, month to month, and with whom it is almost impossible to create a sense of an ongoing story that has a past and a future. The desperate Sunday school teacher looks at his students and thinks, *I have you in my class now and now only, so I'm going to make this as crazy-fun as possible so you come away with something of value, even if it's only the vague notion that Christians can be cool.* But such an approach is not the gospel. It is not the attitude of the storyteller. It gains no traction, no sense of moving forward, no unfolding pattern of transformation. Instead, our ministry should be that of the itinerant preacher or circuit rider—like that of Jesus himself. While he had the people's attention, he gave them stories that would outlast the moment and even outlast his physical presence with them. This is the task of the youth-pastor-as-bard.

RECEIVERS VERSUS USERS

One popular youth ministry handbook says, "We can recover *the story* as the great conveyer of truth, and we can use it to great effect just as Jesus did."[2] Up go all my red flags. Is the story merely *useful*? Is that all it is: one of many communication tools that we can dispense with if we find something that works better? Or is story the very experience we are inviting our listeners to live inside?

C. S. Lewis's classic distinction between good and bad readers in *An Experiment in Criticism* can be helpful in terms of how we approach storytelling with youth. Regarding stories, he says, "To value them chiefly for reflections which they may suggest to us or morals we may draw from them, is a flagrant instance of 'using' instead of 'receiving.'"[3] Art is meant to be experienced, not appropriated for our own purposes. "The first demand any work of any art makes upon us is surrender."[4]

We must be careful about being "users" rather than "receivers" of story, of treating it as merely a useful tool for, say, evangelism, rather than submitting ourselves to the work of the Holy Spirit in our own imaginations as well the imaginations of others. In particular, we must be careful not to *use* the biblical stories but rather *be receivers* of the text. The youth ministry handbook I mentioned earlier suggests, "Let your mind simmer—what could you do with the book of Job? Or with a psalm? Or, to really think outside the box, with Revelation?"[5]—and I can't help wincing. What can we "do" with a text? The better question is, what does the text "do" with us?

> *Storytelling is not a results-based ministry method that can be empirically tracked for effectiveness.*

Likewise, we must be careful not to use or manipulate the listeners. Storytelling is not a results-based ministry method that can be empirically tracked for effectiveness. Respect what the Holy Spirit is doing in the imaginations of your students. Don't try to manipulate, interpret, or explain the story away. You cannot forcibly open ears. Moreover, you may not be around when they finally understand what the story is about—or at least begin to understand it on some level. Allow a story to have multiple layers of meaning, more like an onion than a puzzle. And give your students the freedom and the luxury to unpeel those layers at their own pace.

Storytelling as an art form can be an act of worship in which God is the audience. Worship, we must continually be reminded, is not meant to be "useful"—and if it is, then we must question what we are using it for. True, there's a pragmatism about our gospel mission; but we're also living inside of a tremendous mystery that is epic and extravagant and hugely impractical. We can't quantify it or explain it or even "use" it; we can only invite others in.

MAKING ROOM FOR MYSTERY

For whatever reason, we Christians are willing to acknowledge and even proclaim "the mystery of faith" in every arena of the church except youth ministry. Even the least dogmatic among us youth workers feels pressured to speak in absolutes to the teenagers in our charge, and the youth themselves seem to both demand and resist this at the same time. Parents expect us to teach their children the bald facts of faith, just as they expect the school health teacher to instruct their children in the facts of life. We are, after all, the experts. The congregation hired us to pass the faith on to the next generation because we can "speak their language," which means we're supposedly the least likely to founder in ambiguities and be misunderstood.

Yet all the while our weekly liturgies call each of us, young and old, to "proclaim the mystery of faith: Christ has died; Christ is risen; Christ will come again." Why are we so reticent to proclaim this same mystery when facing a classroom of middle-school boys?

I would suggest this reticence is a uniquely modern attitude that the church must shed if it is to effectively communicate the faith to postmoderns. Much of faith, like life itself, defies logical explanation. What is this strange ceremony we call the Eucharist? It is a sacrament, *mustērion*, a mystery. It's a living experience of Christ-with-us, Christ-in-us that can't empirically be explained. It's a mystery beyond all our attempts to explain it. Honesty requires us to admit so. And if a young adult balks at this response, he or she is not being honest about the nature of human experience itself. But until we operate on the level of mystery ourselves, we can't blame young people for demanding answers and then ditching the whole Christian enterprise when our logical arguments ring hollow.

"EXPERIENTIAL" STORYTELLING: MISSING THE FOREST FOR THE TREES?

When I first pitched the concept for this book to a couple of publishers, one of them said, "Well, have you read *Experiential Storytelling*?" I replied that I hadn't yet. So I read it. The subtitle alone expresses some of my misgivings: *(Re)Discovering Narrative to Communicate God's Message*. As if the story itself isn't what we're really trying to communicate! But the problem with this approach isn't simply its utilitarian view of narrative, but the many exhausting bells and whistles that are required in making a story "experiential." While I hand it to youth workers who go all out, creating whole worlds for their students to live inside, I can't help wondering if we're missing the forest for the trees. At what point does the story get lost in the process of storytelling?

In the midst of my musings on this issue, I came across an online article by a youth worker who voices this very concern: "Students need the power of the Gospel more than they need my flashy PowerPoint presentations. The method of story telling will have no power to transform the next generation unless they hear and believe the message of the Story in the stories we tell them (Galatians 3:1-5)."[6] Amen.

When it comes to our role of youth-pastor-as-bard, once again we must be careful not to confuse *style*—the props, visuals, tech equipment, and so forth—with *form*, with the story's essential thematic structure. We mustn't be drawn into the belief that telling stories to postmoderns should require a lot of extra embellishments, involving all five senses in order to make an impact. Part of the magic of the imagination is that it can conjure something out of nothing except the simple medium of words until the hearer really feels as though she's experiencing a multisensory event. That's the power of the imagination: not that it needs external images, such as PowerPoint slides, photos, or paintings (though these can assist the process), but that it can conjure up those images in the mind's eye with very few raw materials. You'll remember my roomful of hyper confirmands listening to the opening chapter of *The Silver*

Chair by candlelight. My props were as follows: book, candle, matches, darkness.

Especially in teaching the Bible we must be careful not to boil effective storytelling down to a mere quest to make the parables, for example, multisensory. Jesus didn't arrange to have the smell of baking bread in the background when he told the parable about the yeast in the dough. It was the words themselves that held the magic—the way they were crafted and put together into something that conveyed the meaning(s) he intended, not the general atmosphere or emotional delivery. The people remembered the story because it was well told by a worthy storyteller, not because it was experientially embellished by a slide show and seventeen subwoofers.

THE ART OF SUBVERSION

Most days during the week, I attend a traditionally Anglican rite of Morning Prayer. Right now the lectionary is taking us through the book of Acts, and for the first time I've begun to notice how most of the evangelistic messages of the early apostles aren't primarily theological; they're narrative. The apostles stand up in the synagogue or marketplace and start with a story their hearers are familiar with, such as the patriarchs of Israel (Acts 7) or the "unknown god" of Athens (Acts 17). You can almost imagine the Jewish councilmen nodding at Stephen, the Epicureans mouthing the words of their own poets along with Paul. And then quite suddenly, without any warning, the preacher brings Jesus into it.

This is the subversive moment: when the story goes in the exact opposite direction the hearers were expecting. This is why the apostles get jailed or stoned or hauled before various proconsuls and vice-whatevers. Not because they're advancing some kind of propositional argument, but because they're subversive storytellers with a disconcerting penchant for altar calls.

They're downright parabolic, frankly. The word *parable* comes from the Greek *parabole*, which means "to throw alongside" (*para*, "beside, beyond"; *ballein*, "to throw.")[7] It hearkens us back to tenth-grade geometry, when we tracked the arc of a parabola up, up, up one side of the chart and then abruptly down, down, down the other side, till we were no longer going in the same direction we started. Parables are like that. You think they're taking you in one direction, but then suddenly they turn and drag you someplace else entirely. The first will be last; the last will be first.

A few months ago my husband and I found ourselves listening to the radio broadcast of a popular preacher and best-selling author. He made a comment at the beginning of his sermon that brought me up short. "God is on your side," he exhorted his audience; and I immediately thought, *And we wonder why our young people are Moralistic Therapeutic Deists!* Stop for a moment. *Is* God on our side? In the parables, at least, we begin to suspect this may not be the case—unless we are the poor, the disenfranchised, the outcast, the oppressed. A prophet generally tells us what we *don't* want to hear. Meanwhile, the privileged American teenager looks warily at parable because it forces him or her to confront the disquieting question, "What if God *isn't* on my side?"

> *Something more is going on with Jesus' storytelling than clarification or embellishment: he's out to rock our world.*

In parable, the hearer—if he or she grasps any kind of message or takeaway value at all—gains the disconcerting suspicion that the teller isn't who the hearer thought he was. For starters, the teller doesn't seem to be toeing the party line. Nor does he appear to be at all interested in affirming the hearer with a kind of therapeutic camaraderie. There's no sense that the parabler is garnering the hearers' support for some kind of antiestablishment cause by telling them he's on their side. By contrast, he seems to be pushing against both the establishment and the hearer's own popular culture. As Richard Hays puts it, "Jesus' parables are world-disrupting."[8] It's easy to confuse the parables with illustrations, those brief analogies peppered throughout a sermon in order to clarify a point; but that's precisely what they aren't. Something more is going on with Jesus' storytelling than clarification or embellishment: he's out to rock our world.

I've decided that whatever else parables are, they *aren't* universally useful as a teaching method except as a kind of shock treatment for waking up a drowsy class that thinks it's already heard everything the church has to say. A parable doesn't provide a useful framework for understanding a topic, such as the three steps to prayer. Rather, it provides a story-moment that the hearer grasps hold of and tries to anticipate, only to find his or her expectations wildly off the mark before the end. Parable creates an inverse relationship between "the hearer's structure of expectation" and the actual thrust of the story[9]—which makes parable more like riddle than anything else. And how do you "teach" a riddle?

In the end, the youth pastor who chooses to stand in the subversive stream of the prophets and the apostles must be prepared for stonings.

All the same, parables are explorable even if they aren't necessarily teachable. An interesting item to note with a Sunday school class, for example, is the marked contrast between the miraculous nature of Jesus' life and the nonmiraculous nature of the stories he told. In the historical instances we have impossible, fairy tale-like things going on all over the place: dead people wake up, blind men see, coins appear in the mouths of fishes, and so forth. This is not what we expect, so in a way these historical accounts are parabolic. In the parables themselves, meanwhile, we have rarely more than the natural world of vineyards, sheep, and mustard seeds—though the social rules have been turned upside down, and our expectations are thwarted at every turn. Why are Jesus' parables so down-to-earth (albeit disconcerting) while the accounts of his life are so extraordinary (and equally disconcerting)? Mind you: this is not a question of the text's historical reliability. It's a question of form. As a unique form, parable (like satire) is about subversion rather than illustration. And yet, in a way, so are the historical narratives; the Gospel writers are parablers. They're out to disrupt our world, to start a revolution. We either choose to join or we don't.

The parabler makes nobody happy.[10] We really can't blame our young hearers (and their parents) if they're crabby for having been jolted out of a comfy snooze. It's enough to put anyone in a "crucifying mood" (to quote Dorothy Sayers).[11] In the end, the youth pastor who chooses to stand in the subversive stream of the prophets and the apostles must be prepared for stonings.

CLOSING THOUGHTS: FEEDING YOUR OWN GOD-HUNGRY IMAGINATION

Dark intervals aside, at first glance it seems like youth workers have the greatest of jobs. All week long we get to indulge the imagination and binge on story: we're inventing cool metaphors, playing great music, making funky videos, planning poignant skits, creating craft projects, decorating the youth room, and brainstorming ways to engage young minds with the great story of scripture. If we can dream it, we can do it, budget permitting.

The problem is, far too often we lose sight of dreaming for dreaming's sake. When was the last time you read a good novel for your own enjoyment—and didn't somehow work it into an illustration for a youth talk? When did you last jam on the guitar just to make noise? We have many outlets for imaginative creativity in youth ministry, but often we treat them as merely useful means to an educational end: products to serve the purpose of our job description rather than food to nourish the imagination. We are users far more often than we are receivers. So youth are not the only ones whose imaginations are starving.

It took me a few years in full-time ministry to realize how imaginatively malnourished I was. I knew I was tired. I was pretty beat-up emotionally. I was irritated by the demands of parents and kids who just didn't seem to understand my nifty little programmatic formulas. And I was mortified that I couldn't keep my own spiritual life together. But eventually it hit me that part of what I was feeling was imaginative starvation. When was the last time I, a former English major, had read a literary novel? When was the last time I'd taken out my art pens and playfully sketched the little characters I enjoy inventing? And above all, when was the last time I'd read the Bible because I love that timeless, enchanting, strange, and beautiful story?

Right around that time my husband and I headed out west for a long vacation. At the end of the trip we would attend an eight-day small-group retreat at a center for couples in ministry. I knew the trip would be gorgeous, relaxing, and therapeutic—and it was. I also knew I'd have long stretches of time to read, so I planned ahead. Did I bring all the youth ministry resources (like this one) that I always felt so guilty for not reading? Nope. I brought *The Lord of the Rings*. And even though the weather was spectacular that week—and even though wonderful trails and other recreational opportunities were all around us—the only thing I wanted was to walk with Frodo into Mordor. Because if I could live for a little while inside a great story written by a first-rate Christian storyteller, maybe my fragmented world just might make some kind of narrative sense again. And I was right.

So if you're feeling rather fried right now—if the demands of ministry have brought you to the point of imaginative starvation—do yourself a favor. Put down this book and pick up a nice, hefty novel. Sure, it may feel frivolous. It may seem like a waste of time. You may have no way of explaining yourself to the parent from church who happens to call. But it doesn't matter. Right now your primary concern is to remember what it's like to inhabit a narratable world again.

QUESTIONS AND EXERCISES

1. In what context might the bardic-parabolic approach (storytelling) be more appropriate for your ministry with youth than the evangelistic-missional model (straight evangelism)? And vice versa?

2. How easily do you get wrapped up in storytelling (props, equipment, atmospheric embellishments) at the expense of the story

itself? How can you reclaim (or help your leaders and students reclaim) the primacy of the story again?

3. In what ways might you help your students engage with the subversive nature of parable instead of reducing it to mere lesson or illustration? What are the parabolic moments in your ministry?

IDEA FOR THE ROAD

Commit to nourishing your imagination over the next few months by joining a book club, signing up for a community art class, or keeping a guided journal through such creative resources as *The Artist's Way*, by Julia Cameron[12] or *The Creative Call*, by Janice Elsheimer.[13]

FARE FOR THE IMAGINATION

Give ear, O my people, to my teaching;
incline your ears to the words of my mouth.
I will open my mouth in a parable;
I will utter dark sayings from of old,
things that we have heard and known,
that our ancestors have told us.
We will not hide them from their children;
we will tell to the coming generation
the glorious deeds of the LORD, and his might,
and the wonders that he has done.
—Psalm 78:1-4

CHAPTER 9

NOTES FROM THE FIELD

When you can assume that your audience
holds the same beliefs you do, you can relax a
little and use more normal means of talking
to it; when you have to assume that it does not,
then you have to make your vision apparent
by shock.

—FLANNERY O'CONNOR

A couple of years ago I agreed to lead a youth ministry workshop for our annual district leadership retreat. I was told to
submit a title for the workshop by a certain date, but—being
the artsy type—I let it slide, figuring if they didn't get a title from
me on time, they'd simply call it "Youth Ministry Workshop" or
whatever. You can imagine my alarm when the brochure arrived
and I discovered that my talk was titled "Youth: What to Do with
Them"(!). Alas, all the usual misunderstandings about youth
ministry were there: "youth" as an alien culture, a "them" that
leaves the church baffled and undone, and the verb "to do" as the
ultimate response in our purpose-driven culture—all of this pack-
aged into one succinct little statement. But when I apologized to
a conference attendee about the title, she said, "Oh—but that's

why I'm coming to your workshop: I need to know what to *do* with these kids!"

Sigh. All my philosophizing and theologizing can't turn the ship around immediately, I suppose. And the bottom line is that many of us face empty youth rooms each Sunday that slowly fill with middle and high schoolers of all stripes—Moralistic Therapeutic Deists smack in there with I-Don't-Give-a-Damn-ists—and the expectation is that we don't just sit there.

"Redeem the time . . ." a voice whispers in the back of my mind, the voice of a bard speaking to our fears and hopes in the church today. Time is exactly what these kids don't have much of, yet time is exactly what they've given us in this moment. Here at the "still point of the turning world"[1]—in the youth room on a dusky Sunday evening—is where this story we are living either means something or it doesn't. We can't pretend any longer that we know exactly what we're doing, but we know who we are—characters inside the Great Story—and that is enough to drive this plot in a meaningful direction till parents show up to drive these characters home again.

> *Time is exactly what these kids don't have much of, yet time is exactly what they've given us in this moment.*

Obviously, I can't tell you what to "do" with your kids, as if I'm a doctor reading your vitals and then writing a prescription. The best I can do is tell stories from my own youth ministry experience. Some of these story-moments I intuitively stumbled upon; some I actively orchestrated; and some were the Holy Spirit's doing, whether or not I was there to witness them. Many of them were unplanned, which just goes to show how little God is interested in our well-crafted programs or formulas and instead opts for slipping in the unlocked door of imagination when our backs are turned. The trick is staying alert enough to catch what's going on.

If these stories encourage or spark some ideas of your own, then great! And if not—if your first inclination is "this would never fly with my kids"—then pass them by. Remember: I'm just telling stories here, selections from occasional chapters of my experiences in youth ministry.

STORY-MOMENTS

Most of the time church youth activities seem to have little or no narrative structure. We have youth group here, mission trips there, special events here, small groups way over there, and rarely do any of them seem connected to one another, much less to the overall worshiping community. And any attempt at corralling the separate events into some kind of comprehensive youth "program" seems to degenerate into mere formula that never works the same way twice.

Eventually in my own ministry I began to realize that the only way to keep sane was to think of these events as self-contained story-moments. If there was any ongoing narrative woven throughout the year, it would have to happen through corporate worship (which wasn't really up to me), through middle school confirmation, and through high school small groups, because it surely wasn't going to happen in any other way. At least corporate worship would happen every week whether I was involved or not; in confirmation the parents expected their kids to be there consistently; and with small groups, the high schoolers were personally motivated to be there.

In the end I suppose you could say I deconstructed the concept of youth programming altogether and opted for a series of story-moments. But the truth is, the youth program deconstructed itself, and story-moments were all I had left. Here are a few of those.

SUNDAY NIGHT YOUTH GROUP. To be honest, I don't think there was a single program on our regular schedule that I dreaded more. The word *program* says it all. Most of the time I was desperately trying to keep some semblance of order that both welcomed visitors and kept the regulars interested, which meant we usually started with a group-building activity (game, problem solving, etc.) that moved into an interactive "message" followed by a closing prayer circle. Planning the games and the message week after week nearly undid me, because I knew the activities could either fly or die depending on who showed up and what attitude prevailed in the room. But the prayer circle was a gift.

When at the end of the evening I could finally strike a match, light the "Christ candle" (now reclaimed as a symbol of God-with-us rather than of death and loss), and invite their joys and concerns, it was as if we stepped back into the stream of God's grace again. The youth became the storytellers, passing the candle around the circle so each person could share if he or she wished. And they really listened—I mean, really listened. All week long at school, they were playing games and being talked at till they were practically numb. But here at youth group was the only time they heard the heartfelt stories of one another's lives. Here in the darkened church, passing a candle from hand to hand, was the only place they heard grown-ups tell them, "Please pray for me." It was more than just a serendipitous story-moment that put them in the right frame of mind to face the week ahead; it became a much-beloved ritual that grafted our students into the life of the worshiping body.

AREA YOUTH EVENTS. Through a series of fortunate events, the youth groups in our area started doing stuff together. And believe me: in a small town where most of the kids from most churches go to the same school (and where the youth workers generally get along), there's simply no reason to run Lone Ranger youth programs that strain budgets, separate Christian kids from each other, and spread volunteer time and talent far too thin.

First the youth workers started meeting monthly for prayer and encouragement in our separate ministries and events. Then it occurred to us that separate events and even separate ministries were kind of silly. So several of us starting combining our fall retreats (imagine the collective talent of all those trained youth workers and gifted volunteers!), and later we organized a monthly youth-led worship service involving a different church each time. Some of us even began doing youth group together once a month. And the list goes on. It's still going on today.

But one area youth event stood out in my mind as a particularly poignant story-moment. We called it "Go Underground" based on something we found in the Youth Specialties Ideas Library,[2] and it takes place every couple of years or so, to this day. A couple hundred kids show up at a church downtown. They're told that Christianity has now been outlawed. Their job is to follow a series of clues to find safe houses scattered throughout the city where they can worship without getting "arrested." The problem is, the secret police are everywhere—yes, sounds a lot like the game we played at confirmation camp. Got the picture?

So the kids scatter in small groups with their maps and clues. Many get snagged by the secret police and end up back at the church (now transformed into a jail), while the others eventually arrive at safe houses. Their hosts are waiting with snacks and stories about real Christians who are being persecuted around the world today.[3] At the end of the evening, all of the kids, prisoners and free, gather again for a closing worship service.

Admittedly, the first year felt like a disaster. Maps were lost; the secret police were overzealous; some safe houses never saw any kids; and it got dark a lot sooner than expected. By the time closing worship came around, I wasn't surprised to see one girl crying as she limped out of the building with her mom. We leaders quickly intercepted them and asked if everything was okay. "Not to worry," the mom assured us. "Her leg is fine: just on the rebound from an injury. She's crying because she *gets* it. She understands."

Later I heard of kids who sang worship songs while in "prison," boldly admitted they were Christians, and even shared the gospel with their "guards." They had stepped inside a story-moment and found their lives woven together with the strands of Paul and Silas, the cords of secret house churches in China, the threads of Christian refugees in Sudan. It's a moment they would not soon forget. And neither would I.

MISSION TRIPS. I led dozens of these over seven years, for better or worse, but one of the most memorable was a high school trip to Chicago one winter. It was a combined group of Methodists and Presbyterians that we mixed all together and then broke into smaller groups for service projects around the city. On Sunday they could choose to worship at an urban ministry on the north side or at Lawndale Community Church on the south side. Those who chose Lawndale came with me, including a German exchange student named JoJo from the Presbyterian group. Now, JoJo had never in her life experienced anything like Chicago's south side, except in movies; nor had she ever worshiped in the revivalist tradition. She insisted on sitting next to me, ostensibly so I could interpret what was going on. But pretty soon it became clear she needed no interpreter. The vibrant singing, the passionate testimonies, the powerful message—JoJo suddenly found herself immersed in a story and storytelling tradition that knew no cultural barriers. At the end of the service, at the pastor's invitation, she committed her life to Christ. And the few of us who were with her rejoiced and said, "Happy Birthday! You've been born again as a new creation."

But that's not the end of the story-moment. Afterwards we met up with the rest of our group at one of those medieval dinner theaters where everyone gets a paper crown and cheers for their knight in shining armor. Of course, upon entering the lobby, we shared with the rest of the group what had happened to JoJo. Then, as if they'd rehearsed it, one of the waiting adult leaders told her, "Happy Birthday!" and someone else handed her a crown, and we all went into the theater to celebrate JoJo's unplanned but divinely arranged "birthday" party. Could we have told the story any better had we planned it? No, because we weren't the chief storytellers: God was.

SMALL GROUPS. I found Lent to be a great season for weekly small groups. By that time of year only the really die-hard high schoolers are ready to tackle something new (everyone else who showed up for the fun stuff in the fall has gradually drifted away), and Lent gives the group a clear starting and ending point—an important attraction for busy students who can't imagine adding yet one more activity to their schedule. So one year a high school student and her mom decided to do a girls' breakfast club before school. The group consisted of a half dozen, hand-selected postconfirmands along with a few upperclassmen with the gift of encouragement. The mom and I put together a

Lenten devotional that included quotes and excerpts from authors who had touched our lives, and the group discussed each week's readings over breakfast while sharing prayer requests and other issues.

The thing I remember most, besides how tight-knit the group became (we continued meeting weekly for the rest of the school year), was their encounter with a particular Lenten reading that I'd thrown in on a whim. It was a poem by Luci Shaw titled "Royalty." Again, it was one of those random moments of grace in the midst of their usual routine. All week long at school they were being talked at: they read reams of textbook prose and novels for English class, blah, blah, blah. And here was our Lenten study, yet another piece of grown-up blather—except smack in the middle of it was this startling bit of poetry that really got their attention.

Royalty

He was a plain man
and learned no latin

Having left all gold behind
he dealt out peace
to all us wild men
and the weather

He ate fish, bread,
country wine and God's will

Dust sandalled his feet

He wore purple only once
and that was an irony

—Luci Shaw[4]

Of all those forty readings, this was the one that stood out. This was the one they wanted to talk about, though they struggled to find the words. I doubt they usually sat around discussing poetry with their friends. Most likely they'd never seen it modeled by

Christians before. Yet there they were, unpacking irony in the early hours of the morning, trying to fathom how the King of all kings could have been so plain, so dusty, so very ordinary. And what better image to mull over before heading off to plain, dusty, ordinary school in the middle of Lent?

CONFIRMATION AND THE BIG PICTURE

I've already spent significant time on confirmation as a storytelling opportunity in general, but I'd like to touch on confirmation as a *biblical* storytelling opportunity in particular. From infancy our confirmands have heard all kinds of Bible narratives, from Moses parting the Red Sea to Jesus walking on water, but can they tell you which story came first? Can they guess how the two stories are in any way connected? If your answer is yes, then congratulations—sounds like you've got it together. If your answer is no, then you probably can relate to my experience.

I'll never forget the time one of my high school girls, in the middle of a small-group discussion, wailed impatiently, "Wait; stop. I don't get it. Who came first, Jews or Christians?" And this girl had been confirmed (thankfully before my time). And then there was the confirmand in my middle school Sunday school class, who, partway through our multiweek study of King David, blurted out, "Hey, I know! This is *Dave and the Giant Pickle!*"[5] Our youth know their vegetables, but they don't know how the original Bible stories hang together, much less what any of this has to do with them personally. These and similar experiences brought me to the realization that *our main scriptural task in catechesis is not in-depth study on a particular book or topic, but an overall exploration of the Big Picture.*

In chapter 5 I gave examples of ways to explore the Bible-as-story with youth by considering the elements of character (scripture is a "faithful portrait"), tone (the Bible isn't "propaganda"), and form (distinguishing between prose and poetry, etc.). Now let's take a look at plot and setting, both of which I've found to be uniquely suited for articulating the Big Picture.

I'll start with setting. Early in our marriage my husband was rather addicted to a board game called Axis and Allies that replays key World War II military scenarios on a large map of the world. Often I would be drafted to play one side or the other, and in this instance I was the Axis powers squaring off against Britain, which is fairly easy to squash if you annihilate its naval fleet. But it's not so easy to defeat if it manages to build an industrial complex on Israel, which is exactly what my husband did. From that tiny little anchor in the Middle East, he was able to send troops, ships, and planes—in just a few moves—to any continent on the playing field (with the exception of the Americas, which aren't really part of the game). My guys were getting smashed in Africa, Asia, and Europe; and meanwhile I was learning the hard way what the ancient superpowers knew: if you own Israel, you own the gateway to the world.

Once my kids grasped the importance of setting, they could begin to make sense of the overarching biblical plot.

So you can guess what I did. Sure enough, the board game went to confirmation camp, where I spread out the map, set up the pieces, and replayed the scene. After describing my crushing defeat, I said, "Now let's pretend it's 2000 BC. The Americas aren't even in the picture yet, so what are the three main continents of the known world? Right: Europe, Asia, and Africa. And where do those three continents all come together? Yep, they all converge on this tiny little spot on the Mediterranean Sea. So if you were an ancient superpower and wanted to have access to everything, what would you need to do? Absolutely: control this spot. And if you were God, and you wanted the known world to hear the story of salvation, where would you put your messengers?"

Pretty simple, really. There is a method to the geographical madness of the ancient world, baldly speaking, and once my kids grasped the importance of setting, they could begin to make sense of the overarching biblical plot (along with what's happening on the nightly news). They could begin to see why Abraham was sent on his journey, why Moses crossed the Red Sea, why David was such a great king, why Daniel was in so much trouble, why Jesus was born in Bethlehem of Judea, and why Paul was so well suited to be the first Christian missionary. The whole exercise took about twenty minutes, though it goes without saying there were some new Axis and Allies addicts before camp was over. And why not? Every time they play the game from now on, they'll remember why Israel is so important in the biblical narrative.

Now we turn to plot. As it became clear that our confirmands didn't have a handle on the Master Narrative—particularly what the Old Testament has to do with anything—I created a story-moment that I began to call "The Old Testament in Forty-five Minutes." Ahead of time, on separate pieces of colored construction paper, I wrote simple summaries of key Bible stories, starting with "God created everything" all the way to "Nehemiah returns with the exiles to rebuild Jerusalem." In between I put the main characters from the key eras in red: Abraham for the Ancestors, Moses for the Exodus, David for the Kingdom, and Daniel for the Exile.[6] Then I shuffled the papers and distributed them at random to the confirmands. Their instructions were: "Your group task is to put these stories together, as best you can, into an Old Testament time line. The trick is, *there's no talking.* And you may not snatch a paper from someone's hands: the person must offer it to the group. Last year's class did this in ten minutes: I'll time you to see if you can beat them. Ready? One, two, three, go."

And off they went. It was intriguing to watch. I could tell immediately which kids had some sense of the ongoing biblical narrative and which ones were clueless. Soon they all were on hands and knees, spreading the growing time line out on the floor, miming their arguments and agreements, scratching their heads over the stories they'd never heard. When time was up, I took over. First, I made sure they knew that Israel's history is divided into four key eras—Patriarchs, Exodus, Kingdom, and Exile—and I had them say the eras over and over, in that order, till they knew them by heart. Then I told them that the main character from each era is on a red sheet of paper. I said, "Once you have these guys in the right order, most everything else falls into place. For example, if this particular story mentions a king in Israel, which era is it most likely to be? And if this story has something to do with Egypt, when did it most likely take place?" So of course the kids tracked down the red sheets and determined whether or not the key characters were in the correct order, and then started rearranging things accordingly. All told, they had the Old Testament put together in roughly forty-five minutes.

Of course, I doubted whether they'd still remember it a month or even a day afterwards, so one year I did a test. I invited any campers who wanted to do "extra credit" during free time to take me aside and put the time line together on their own (the reward was a brand-new Super Soaker). One girl wasn't interested in waiting till the person who preceded her was finished; so she took out a blank sheet of paper, divided it into four sections, labeled each section according to the key biblical eras, and handwrote everything she could remember in between. Needless to say, she got a Super Soaker. The rest of us got wet.

Not incidentally, the time-line exercise worked so well that our pastor and I decided to do the same thing with church history. That's when it gets really interesting. They know where to put Martin Luther King Jr., but what about *Martin Luther*?[7]

The Big Picture isn't difficult for our kids to understand. They've just never heard how all the stories hang together. Part of our job as resident bards is to help them weave together the loose ends of what they already know.

NOTES FROM ABROAD

By now you're probably wondering why I'm not in full-time youth ministry anymore if I clearly loved it so much. The answer is complicated, obviously, and has a lot to do with Frodo. But even as my husband and I find ourselves in a new town while pursuing graduate school, we also find ourselves in an urban church that hasn't had a confirmation class in years. So guess who has been drafted to help start one? Yep. And I'm excited by the opportunity, even as I recognize the challenges it holds.

We've talked about the catechetical process as a cultural-linguistic adventure for the catechumens who are learning the Christian language and way of life. Well, this time I'll be a catechumen too, even as I'm a catechist (one of several). That's because my new worshiping community is a historically African-American church that comes from both a liturgical and a revivalist heritage, which means the storytelling well runs deep, deep, deep. In worship, the call-and-response form of proclamation and song makes every person there a storyteller, not just the pastor or the worship leaders. The music tells a story; the prayers tell a story; the personal testimonies tell a story. And most importantly, the scriptures tell *our* story, not some dusty old tale from thousands of years ago. We're living it right now, hence the prophetic tone to much African-American preaching.

So I'm learning by immersion. And even though I come from a different cultural-linguistic context than the students and leaders who are part of confirmation, our story is the same: Once we were not a people, but now we are God's people (1 Pet. 2:10); once we had no story, but now we live God's story. We are storytellers together.

CLOSING THOUGHTS

If I've learned one thing about the art of storytelling for postmodern ministry, it's that you can't really measure the results. There's no empirical data that helps you track whether imaginations were engaged, ears were opened, narrative connections made. It's a those-who-have-ears-let-them-hear kind of enterprise. Which is why the usual youth ministry rhetoric about "measurable success" and "standards of excellence" seems jarring to me. What about a "standard of faithfulness" instead? Faithfulness to the story. Faithfulness to the hearers. Faithfulness to the art of storytelling itself, which began long before we got here and will continue long after we're gone. And most importantly, faithfulness to our central character, Jesus, whose words will never pass away.

In the end, the story we inhabit is not one of continual progress toward an achievable goal, like Bilbo in *The Hobbit*, who is "there and back again" with a ponyload of treasure. It's not a story of success (successful ministries, budgets, buildings, memberships, numbers), mission accomplished. Rather it's one in which tragedy, loss, and lack of traction are inevitable—more like Frodo in *The Lord of the Rings*, who comes home wounded in mind and body. It's one in which the sheep more often scatter than are gathered in the fold, where the shepherd must continually leave the ninety-nine pew sitters—with their buildings and programs and budgets and numbers—to go the lonely path after the Moralistic Therapeutic Deist who is lost. In the end it's not a story of success at all but of fidelity: "the marital promise of faithfulness unto death."[8]

This is the story we're inviting others into, the story Jesus lived and told; this is the story we weave together as youth minister-bards in a postmodern world.

Those who have ears, let them hear!

QUESTIONS AND EXERCISES

1. When do you feel the most pressure to "do" something with the youth in your church? How might a storytelling approach to ministry alleviate some of that pressure?

2. How well do your students know the "Big Picture" of the Bible? What might you do to help them make meaningful connections between the stories they already know?

3. How helpful is it to think of your church's overall youth ministry as a series of "story-moments" rather than an attempt at formulaic "youth programming"? When are the story-moments in your ministry?

IDEA FOR THE ROAD

Find some youth ministry colleagues in your area with whom you can meet regularly for prayer and support. Consider working through this or another youth ministry resource as a way to brainstorm how your churches might work intentionally together in creating story-moments for the youth in your community. But more importantly, encourage one another in your roles as resident bards. It's not easy out there!

FARE FOR THE IMAGINATION

There is a certain embarrassment about being a storyteller in these times when stories are considered not quite as satisfying as statements and statements not quite as satisfying as statistics; but in the long run, a people is known, not by its statements or its statistics, but by the stories it tells.

—FLANNERY O'CONNOR[9]

APPENDIX A

"IMAGINATIVE INTELLIGENCE"?

For those of us who find ourselves cleaning up pencil shards after what feels like yet another fruitless seventh-grade Sunday school class, it's encouraging to know there are smart people in the fields of developmental psychology and education who are trying to help us understand what's going on. It's also encouraging to know that many of those people take both faith and imagination seriously.

Several who have explored the role of the imagination in the moral or spiritual formation of adolescents include James W. Fowler with his stages of faith development (*Stages of Faith: The Psychology of Human Development*); Robert Coles with "moral imagination" (*The Moral Intelligence of Children*); and John H. Westerhoff III with "owned faith" (*Will Our Children Have Faith?*).[1] Educators such as Maria Harris have also made helpful contributions to discussions about religious imagination (*Teaching and Religious Imagination*).[2]

But since we've already discussed the imagination as a faculty of the intellect—a kind of intelligence, if you will—perhaps we should see how it might interface with Multiple Intelligences Theory, a concept developed by Harvard psychologist Howard Gardner and outlined in his landmark book *Frames of Mind: The Theory of Multiple Intelligences*.[3] The seven intelligences he discusses are not so much learning styles as they are natural abilities or "smarts." They include verbal-linguistic, logical-mathematical, body-kinesthetic, visual-spatial, auditory-musical, interpersonal communication, and intra-personal communication.[4] Despite the controversial and somewhat fluid nature of this theory (new additions to the list are suggested all the time, including "spiritual intelligence"), educators for the past twenty years have found it helpful to take different kinds of intelligence into account as they teach. This includes Christian educators, as witnessed by Barbara Bruce's *Seven Ways of Teaching the Bible to Children*,[5] even though Gardner himself is reluctant to go the spiritual route.

Now, this may sound cheeky, but given our considerations up to this point, I'd like to propose as Christian educators we add *imaginative intelligence* to the list. If we embrace the classical definition of the imagination as a faculty of the intellect, it would certainly seem plausible to suggest that someone could have imaginative intelligence, here defined as *the intuitive ability to discover and express meaningful relationships and patterns between otherwise unconnected ideas, images, and experiences*—or the ability to put things together. Such ability might be expressed through a gift for metaphor, word pictures, world building, narrative, poetry, parable, and even prophecy, but it may also include visual arts or intuitive problem solving (as in, "I've figured out why this fits together, but I can't logically explain how"). This kind of intelligence shares some characteristics with verbal-linguistic, visual-spatial, and intrapersonal communication but is unique in terms of apprehending patterns of *meaning*, not simply visual or linguistic or internal patterns.

Perhaps you can think of several students in your church or youth ministry who seem naturally equipped with this kind of intelligence while defying all other categories. My Indiana Jones impersonator from confirmation camp comes to mind (see chapter 7). As Christian educators, how might we offer experiences that touch upon this kind of "smarts"?

APPENDIX B

FURTHER MUSINGS ON THE BIBLE AND NARRATIVE FORM

Several years ago I read a recap of a mainline youth convention in which, according to the reporter, the students in one particular workshop were shocked to learn that Job is supposedly a work of fiction. Job wasn't the topic of the workshop, so I guess the facilitator probably tossed that comment out there as a throwaway aside but suddenly found, to his dismay, that the casual rhetoric of seminary doesn't translate very well to an audience of middle schoolers. Words have power, and "fiction" in this context is a hand grenade. No matter how you spin it, to the average American it means "untrue." Period.

Youth today, however postmodern they may be in other areas, still judge a story's trustworthiness according to its scientific and historical accuracy—*when* that story purports to be true. And they're particularly shaken when things that purport to be facts turn out to be fictions. This to them is the highest form of deception and betrayal, and, when applied to the biblical texts, has severe theological implications. We can't blithely assume their relationship with the Word of God—and thus with the person of God—will remain untouched by questions of "reliability." But there's also the sticky issue of integrity in what and how we teach. If we honestly think that straight journalism or even historical accuracy is not the point of a biblical narrative, then why should we hide this from our students?

Okay, let's take a deep breath and think about everything we've discussed so far. Obviously, it's important to be clear on what literary form we're working with when discussing biblical stories with youth, whether poetry, epistle, parable, and so forth. But we must also be clear on this: just because a narrative (such as the book of Job) falls within the limitations and devices of a certain artistic form (such as opera) doesn't therefore make the narrative "fictional" (e.g., not based on actual events). As my husband, a former statistics assistant, is fond of telling me, "Correlation does not mean causation." It merely means that the storyteller(s) chose opera as the form by which they would tell their tale, just as Andrew Lloyd Webber and Tim Rice chose Broadway musical as the form by which they would tell the story of Argentine actress and labor activist Eva Perón.

Did Evita actually, factually dance with Antonio Banderas onstage somewhere in Buenos Aires? We can hazard a guess that this is a fictional element within the movie version of the musical. But the historical figure Evita did "dance" with the hearts of Argentine laborers, metaphorically speaking, in which case the musical can be seen as a "faithful portrait" of her character. Of course, musical as a form isn't in the business of historicity to begin with; the audience is aware of that. And yet, if I were a laborer in a developing country, it would be small comfort to be told that, based on the narrative devices employed in the musical *Evita*, experts have concluded that she didn't actually *exist*. We must never forget that form tells us little or nothing about the historical veracity of the tale itself.

Enter our poor workshop leader at the youth convention. We can affirm his sense that if we're going to teach with integrity, we must tell our students that very few biblical narratives are interested in giving us just the bald facts like the front page of *The Free Press*. There is more intended and more at stake than straight journalism. But at the same time and for the same reason, it's important to steer clear of the word *fiction* as the only other alternative.

In fact, given the limitations and devices of opera as a form, we dare not say for certain that Job *didn't* really exist or suffer the things that happened to him.

Take Shakespeare's *Macbeth* as another example. Many people have resonated with and been disturbed by the timeless tragedy, even as they thought Macbeth and his creepy wife were purely fictional products of the Bard's creative genius. But scholars suspect that Macbeth was in fact a historical character who in other ancient texts goes by the name of Thorfinn.[1] It's a fairly credible claim that lends an even creepier pall to the whole drama. Even today, much that we call "fiction" is in fact a fictionalized version of historical events, told within the limitations and devices of various literary forms. As most novelists will tell you, there really is no such thing as "pure" fiction anyway. Our inspiration comes from somewhere, and more often than not it comes from a scenario near at hand. Shakespeare most likely wasn't interested in historical accuracy, but he very likely was interested in his neighbors.

The example of Macbeth begs the question as to whether or not it really matters if we call any story purely fictional—after all, audiences have enjoyed the play for four hundred years without needing the extra bit of historical insight that might lead them to think otherwise. And I'm not sure it does matter one way or the other, because in Shakespeare "the play's the thing." But when it comes to biblical narratives, I suggest it does matter. To casually call anything in the Bible "fiction" is not the same as calling it *literary* or even *fictionalized*; it's a statement of historical accuracy, at least to the hearers, and derails the conversation into the very mess we'd hoped to avoid. If we can't say for certain that Job *didn't* exist, then why risk a child losing his or her faith over it?

And then, of course, there's the obvious issue of divine inspiration, which (I need hardly remind us) has been held as orthodox Christian belief for two thousand years. As we already said, authors receive their ideas from *somewhere*; and in the case of holy scriptures, that *somewhere* is the mind of God. Human beings encountered Someone outside of their ordinary, everyday experience; and that Someone provided both the source and the interpretive lens for the way those encounters were narrated. So, literary concerns aside, we're wandering into very dangerous waters indeed when we suggest to a young person that both the source and the lens of any biblical narrative is somehow unreliable—which is exactly what we're saying, whether we intend it or not, when we label it "fiction." (And what was that pithy statement Jesus made about a millstone . . .?)

We are faithful storytellers in a long line of faithful storytellers who recognize that words have power. We must know what we're about.

APPENDIX C

SUGGESTED RESOURCES

All kinds of cool things are happening for youth ministers who want to take story seriously. Here's just a taste.

GOOD STUFF FOR STORYTELLING

Claremont School of Theology's **Narrative Pedagogies Project** (www.cst.edu/academic_resources/narrative_pedogogies.php) was headed by Dr. Frank Rogers. Says the Web site: "The purpose of the Narrative Pedagogies Project is to cultivate youth for Christian leadership using the narrative art forms of storytelling, creative writing, and drama."

The Catechesis of the Good Shepherd (www.cgsusa.org), originally created by theologian Sofia Cavalletti in Italy, is a way of teaching Bible stories to small children, based on the Montessori method. Both Jerome Berryman of *Godly Play* (www.godlyplay.org) and Sonja Stewart of *Young Children and Worship* (www.childrenandworship.org) were trained in this method and developed it for their unique settings (Episcopal and Reformed, respectively). So I wonder: what if we were to train older youth in becoming storytellers to younger children through these methods?

The Network of Biblical Storytellers (www.nobs.org) provides training in the traditional folk art of oral storytelling and then gathers occasionally throughout the year for workshops and conferences. They consider biblical storytelling both a spiritual discipline and a liturgical art. Many of them are available to bring their storytelling to churches for worship, retreats, and other special events.

The Youth & Family Institute (www.youthandfamilyinstitute.org) has many hands-on resources, including Faith Talk Cards and the Milestones Blessing Bowl, both of which are designed to get adults and youth talking together about important memories, stories, values, and beliefs.

FILM, DRAMA, AND AUDIO RESOURCES

Radio Theatre audio dramas from Focus on the Family (www.radiotheatre.org) include some great classics, such as *At the Back of the North Wind* by George MacDonald and *Les Misérables* by Victor Hugo.

The Strangely Warmed Players youth drama troupe from First United Methodist Church of Ann Arbor, Michigan, directed by Beth Miller; www.fumc-a2.org/strangely_warmed.cfm. Fifteen of their dramas are published in Abingdon's Worship Feast resources (see page 183).

www.lumicon.org. The mission of Lumicon, according to the Web site, is "to empower and equip the church to use the language and tools of digital culture through worship resources and education." Includes a lectionary-based index.

www.nooma.com. Created by Rob Bell, the poster child for emergent preaching, these original film clips are, essentially, narrated metaphors designed to illuminate a spiritual point. Best for classes or small groups but can be used in worship.

www.textweek.com/movies/movies.htm. A fairly exhaustive index of visual art and film clips corresponding to biblical and lectionary-based themes or topics.

www.visualscripture.com. Film shorts that pair scripture with images and text, rather like a video version of a PowerPoint slide show.

GROUP STUDY RESOURCES FOR CHILDREN AND YOUNGER TEENS

Faerie Gold: Treasures from the Lands of Enchantment, a collection of classic fairy tales edited by Kathryn Lindskoog and Ranelda Mack Hunsicker (Phillipsburg, NJ: P&R Publishing, 2005). A guide for teachers and students is also available.

Progeny Press's literature study guides for various age levels are geared for Christian homeschooling but can be adapted for Sunday school classes or small groups. See www.progenypress.com.

Swallowing the Golden Stone: Stories and Essays, by Walter Wangerin Jr. (Minneapolis: Augsburg Books, 2001), includes short stories and poems interspersed with thoughtful essays on the power of story.

Walking with Bilbo: A Devotional Adventure through The Hobbit, by Sarah Arthur (Wheaton, IL: Tyndale House Publishers, 2005), includes suggested scriptures and questions for reflection and discussion.

Walking through the Wardrobe: A Devotional Quest into The Lion, the Witch and the Wardrobe, by Sarah Arthur (Wheaton, IL: Tyndale House Publishers, 2005), was an official church resource of Walden Media's *The Chronicles of Narnia: The Lion, the Witch and the Wardrobe*.

GROUP STUDY RESOURCES FOR YOUTH AND ADULTS

Image: A Journal of the Arts and Religion is a quarterly publication edited by Gregory Wolfe, writer-in-residence and director of the

MFA in Creative Writing at Seattle Pacific University. Each issue includes essays, fiction, poetry, full color art plates, and music and book reviews. A quarterly discussion guide is available at www.imagejournal.org/studyguide.

Progeny Press's literature study guides include sophisticated materials for high school students (see previous section).

Walking with Frodo: A Devotional Journey through The Lord of the Rings, by Sarah Arthur (Wheaton, IL: Tyndale House Publishers, 2003).

GROUP STUDY RESOURCES FOR YOUTH WORKERS AND PASTORS

The Godbearing Life: The Art of Soul Tending for Youth Ministry, by Kenda Creasy Dean and Ron Foster (Nashville, TN: Upper Room Books, 1998). Still a youth ministry classic!

Developing a Christian Imagination: An Interpretive Anthology, compiled by Warren W. Wiersbe (Wheaton, IL: Victor Books, 1995). This is a companion to his textbook *Preaching and Teaching with Imagination: The Quest for Biblical Ministry* (Grand Rapids, MI: Baker Books, 1994).

RESOURCES FOR PERSONAL GROWTH AND MINISTRY

The Christian Imagination: The Practice of Faith in Literature and Writing, rev. ed., ed. Leland Ryken (Colorado Springs, CO: WaterBrook Press, 2002). Includes essays, quotes, and excerpts on art, literature, and story from such notables as Annie Dillard, Flannery O'Connor, J. R. R. Tolkien, C. S. Lewis, Frederick Buechner, T. S. Eliot, and more. It's one of the most definitive anthologies of Christian thinking on the subject of faith and literature.

Cloud of Witnesses audio journals produced by Princeton Theological Seminary Institute for Youth Ministry; specifically, Volume 5: Play and Volume 6: Story.
www.ptsem.edu/iym/publications/witnesses/index.htm.

How to Read the Bible as Literature: And Get More Out of It, by Leland Ryken (Grand Rapids, MI: Zondervan, 1985). Succinct and accessible; a beginner's guide.

Introducing the Uncommon Lectionary: Opening the Bible to Seekers and Disciples, by Thomas G. Bandy (Nashville, TN: Abingdon Press, 2006). Bandy "lays out a plan for a trip through the central biblical narratives, the purpose of which is to provide seekers with a basic understanding of the gospel, and to call disciples to a deeper experience of Christian faith."

The Storyteller's Companion to the Bible series, ed. Michael E. Williams (Nashville, TN: Abingdon Press). The side-notes based on midrashic commentary on the biblical text are fabulous.

Worship Feast resources, including *50 Complete Multisensory Services for Youth; 100 Awesome Ideas for Postmodern Youth;* and *15 Sketches for Youth Group, Worship, and More* (Nashville, TN: Abingdon Press, 2003).

NOTES

OPENING EPIGRAPH

Robert Penn Warren, "Tell Me a Story," in *New and Selected Poems, 1923–1985* (New York: Random House, 1985), 230.

PREFACE

1. Kenda Creasy Dean and Ron Foster, *The Godbearing Life: The Art of Soul Tending for Youth Ministry* (Nashville, TN: Upper Room Books, 1998).

2. Ibid., 15.

3. Christian Smith with Melinda Lundquist Denton, *Soul Searching: The Religious and Spiritual Lives of American Teenagers* (New York: Oxford University Press, 2005).

4. Ibid., 131.

PART I: POSTMODERN MINISTRY

INTRODUCTION TO PART I

Epigraph. Frederick Buechner, *The Alphabet of Grace* (San Francisco: Harper-SanFrancisco, 1989), 51.

CHAPTER I: A "NARRATABLE WORLD"?

Epigraph. Madeleine L'Engle Herself: Reflections on a Writing Life, Carole F. Chase, comp. (Colorado Springs, CO: WaterBrook Press, 2001), 343.

1. C. S. Lewis, *On Stories: And Other Essays on Literature* (San Diego: Harcourt, 1982), 47.

2. Robert W. Jenson, "How the World Lost Its Story," *First Things* 36 (October 1993): 19–24. Accessed at: http://print.firstthings.com/ftissues/ft9310/articles/jenson.html.

3. *Four Views on Salvation in a Pluralistic World*, ed. Dennis L. Okholm and Timothy R. Phillips (Grand Rapids, MI: Zondervan, 1996).

4. William C. Placher, introduction to *Theology and Narrative: Selected Essays*, by Hans W. Frei (New York: Oxford University Press, 1993), 19.

5. Jenson, "How the World Lost Its Story."

6. Smith and Denton, *Soul Searching*, 131 (emphasis theirs).

7. A phrase suggested to C. S. Lewis by his friend Owen Barfield and used regularly by Lewis (e.g., see *An Experiment in Criticism* [Cambridge: Cambridge University Press, first published 1961; 2004], 73).

8. Smith and Denton, *Soul Searching*, 162–63.

9. Ibid., 175.

10. See Paul West, *The Secret Lives of Words* (New York: Harcourt, 2000), 207.

11. Ray Buckley, *Dancing with Words: Storytelling as Legacy, Culture, and Faith* (Nashville, TN: Discipleship Resources, 2003), 42.

12. I must offer one caveat, which is to acknowledge that throughout this book I play fast and loose with the term *storytelling*. There's a vocation and folk art of storytelling that trains a gifted person to speak in a particular oral tradition to audiences for the purposes of inspiring, educating, entertaining, or touching the inner spirit. This is a unique and highly skilled calling. Of these trained storytellers—many of whom have graduate degrees in the art—I am in awe, and I do not wish to diminish what they do by using a broader definition. As youth workers, we can learn much from the official storytellers in how to become skilled ourselves. Some of us will want to train as they have done. But until then we must never think we have become masters at a folk art that takes years of training—unless we're willing to go through the same processes of certification through such groups as the Network of

Biblical Storytellers (see Appendix C for more information).

13. Ellen F. Davis, *Imagination Shaped: Old Testament Preaching in the Anglican Tradition* (Valley Forge, PA: Trinity Press International, 1995), xii.

14. Smith and Denton, *Soul Searching*, 267–68.

PART 2: IMAGINATION

INTRODUCTION TO PART 2

1. *The Lord of the Rings.*

2. "A Elbereth Gilthoniel" is a sort of prayer in one of Tolkien's invented Elvish languages. See book 4, chapter 10 of *The Lord of the Rings: The Two Towers.*

3. See Lewis's opening essay in the Eerdmans edition of George MacDonald's *Phantastes: A Faerie Romance* (Grand Rapids, MI: William B. Eerdmans Publishing Company, 1981), xi.

4. See *The Letters of J. R. R. Tolkien,* ed. Humphrey Carpenter (Boston: Houghton Mifflin Company, 2000), 243.

CHAPTER 2: DEFINING IMAGINATION

Epigraph. J. K. Rowling, *Harry Potter and the Sorcerer's Stone* (New York: Scholastic Press, 1998), 5.

1. A title given to nonmagical folk in the Harry Potter series.

2. Alas, in theological studies, definitions of imagination are rare and surprisingly vague. As Garrett Green has shown in *Imagining God: Theology and the Religious Imagination* (San Francisco: Harper & Row, 1989), philosophers on the "Hegelian Left" were the first culprits, essentially equating religion *with* imagination, or rather calling it a *product* of the imagination: something imaginary or illusory. As I say in the main text, "even now there's a tenacious tendency among both liberals and conservatives to equate imagination with making stuff up." I suppose this makes sense, given their modernist heritage. If old-school liberals were the first to discuss imagination as an element in the spiritual enterprise—taking their cues first from Enlightenment philosophy and then from Freud—then naturally conservatives would have revolted from any association with the term. On this, perhaps

more than any other, issue we see the liberal tendency to give human beings too much credit and the conservative tendency to give too little. In the one view, our ancestors were imaginative geniuses of epic and pathological proportions, while in the other they had the visionary abilities of a slug.

3. At best, theologians equate imagination with vision—the ability to visualize spiritual reality and one's relationship to it—and/or they equate imagination with worldview, the cultural lens through which one views and understands the world. Yet worldview doesn't account for those instances when a text crashes uninvited into your world and radically confronts your way of seeing. Vision, meanwhile, is a new way of seeing that then prompts the will to action. But how did you arrive at that new way of seeing? Vision in particular seems to be an important element of what the imagination makes possible, but again I would argue this doesn't necessarily define imagination.

4. See Donald T. Williams's essay "Christian Poetics, Past and Present" in *The Christian Imagination*, rev. ed., Leland Ryken, ed. (Colorado Springs, CO: WaterBrook Press, 2002), 3–22.

5. Ellen F. Davis, *Wondrous Depth: Preaching the Old Testament* (Louisville, KY: Westminster John Knox Press, 2005),149.

6. Green, *Imagining God*, 40. Hurrah for the scholars and theologians after all!

7. J. R. R. Tolkien, "On Fairy-Stories," from *The Tolkien Reader* (New York: Ballantine Books, 1966), 75.

8. Dorothy L. Sayers, *The Mind of the Maker* (San Francisco: Harper-SanFrancisco, 1987), 22.

9. "The Imagination: Its Functions and Its Culture," in *The Heart of George MacDonald*, ed. Rolland Hein (Vancouver, BC: Regent College Publishing, 2004), 416.

10. *The Tolkien Reader*, 68.

11. See chapter 13, "On the Imagination, or Esemplastic Power," in Coleridge's *Biographia Literaria: Or Biographical Sketches of My Literary Life and Opinions*, ed. George Watson (London: J. M. Dent & Sons, 1975), 167.

12. See Appendix A for my playful exploration of "imaginative

intelligence" as a possible addition to Howard Gardner's multiple intelligence theory.

13. *The Heart of George MacDonald*, 416.

14. David F. White, *Practicing Discernment with Youth: A Transformative Youth Ministry Approach* (Cleveland, OH: Pilgrim Press, 2005), 121.

15. Coleridge's concept of the "primary imagination" would suggest that it is God who is the ultimate Meaning-Maker; we, as secondary creatures with our secondary imaginations, are the ones who are the Meaning-Discoverers. God is the one who brings elements together; establishes order; makes connections; draws boundaries; and playfully creates patterns of light, sound, color, and shape—all according to a certain divine sense that invests what we see with meaning. We humans are merely witnesses and discoverers of that meaning. We cannot create something out of nothing, but we can create something out of the something God has given us. The imagination in this context strikes a backhanded blow at the existentialism and nihilism of our postmodern era while at the same time recognizing that not all meaning has yet been discovered or revealed. God likes to play hide-and-seek.

16. *Selected Literary Essays*, ed. Walter Hooper (Cambridge: Cambridge University Press, 1979), 265.

17. Despite our general view of C. S. Lewis as one of the greatest Christian apologists of the twentieth century—a master at logical argument who built a reasonable defense of the faith—his view of the imagination pushes against the modern Enlightenment model that would place reason at the pinnacle of human experience. This isn't to say he elevates imagination over reason: far from it. But he takes issue with the modern emphasis on reason even as he steps into the apologetic fray with flashing sword. Was he a postmodern? No, he was an ex-modern who, like Tolkien, ditched his youthful "chronological snobbery" in favor of an older, more medieval worldview. Lewis's attempts to balance reason and imagination resulted in some of the most potent apologetics and profoundly imaginative fiction the church produced in the twentieth century. And since that struggle was at the heart of his reluctant conversion to Christianity (see his autobiography, *Surprised by Joy*), he also gave us an important

glimpse into the vital role of the imagination in spiritual formation—a glimpse that proves to be a crack in a door that, once opened, leads to a vast and marvelous new world.

18. From the sermon "Christ and the Imagination," first published in 1909; reprinted in Warren Wiersbe's *Developing a Christian Imagination: An Interpretive Anthology* (Wheaton, IL: Victor Books, 1995), 70.

19. Green, *Imagining God*, 73.

20. A concept C. S. Lewis explores in the essay mentioned earlier: "Bluspels and Flalansferes," from *Selected Literary Essays*.

21. Sayers, *The Mind of the Maker*, 23.

22. Hans W. Frei, *Types of Christian Theology*, ed. George Hunsinger and William C. Placher (New Haven, CT: Yale University Press, 1992), 140.

23. *The Heart of George MacDonald*, 419.

CHAPTER 3: IMAGINATION AND SPIRITUAL FORMATION

Epigraph. "In Praise of Stories," in *The Christian Imagination*, 422.

1. More on this in chapter 7.

2. Green, *Imagining God*, 101.

3. Smith and Denton, *Soul Searching*, 165.

4. Green, *Imagining God*, 90.

5. "On Fairy-stories," in *The Tolkien Reader*, 79.

6. Ibid.

7. Sayers, *The Mind of the Maker*, 145.

8. See Ryken's essay "With Many Such Parables: The Imagination as a Means of Grace," in Warren W. Wiersbe's anthology, *Developing a Christian Imagination*.

9. Peter J. Schakel, *Imagination and the Arts in C. S. Lewis: Journeying to Narnia and Other Worlds* (Columbia, MO: University of Missouri Press, 2002), 164.

10. "The Christian Imagination," in *The Christian Imagination*, 66.

11. Walter Wangerin Jr., "Hans Christian Andersen: Shaping the Child's Universe," in *More Than Words: Contemporary Writers on the Works That Shaped Them*, comp. Philip Yancey, ed. James Calvin Schaap (Grand Rapids, MI: Baker Books, 2002), 133.

PART 3: STORY

INTRODUCTION TO PART 3

1. From Lewis, *The Silver Chair*, 159.

CHAPTER 4: WHAT IS STORY, AND WHY DOES IT WORK?

Epigraph. Flannery O'Connor, *Mystery and Manners: Occasional Prose*, ed. Sally and Robert Fitzgerald (New York: Farrar, Straus & Giroux, 1970), 96.

1. I'm indebted to both Leland Ryken (*How to Read the Bible as Literature: And Get More out of It*) and Madeleine L'Engle (*Walking on Water: Reflections on Faith and Art*) for this understanding of story.

2. See Joseph Campbell's *The Hero with a Thousand Faces* (Princeton, NJ: Princeton University Press, 2004); originally published 1949.

3. See Christopher Vogler, *The Writer's Journey: Mythic Structure for Writers* (Studio City, CA: Michael Wiese Productions, 1998).

4. Tolkien, *The Letters of J. R. R. Tolkien*, 243.

5. Frei, *The Eclipse of the Biblical Narrative: A Study in Eighteenth and Nineteenth Century Hermeneutics* (New Haven, CT: Yale University Press, 1974), 11.

6. O'Connor, *Mystery and Manners*, 129.

7. Buckley, *Dancing with Words*, 11.

8. Ibid., 54-55.

9. Lucy Pevensie in *The Lion, the Witch and the Wardrobe* by C. S. Lewis, chapter 1.

10. Madeleine L'Engle, *Walking on Water: Reflections on Faith and Art* (Colorado Springs, CO: WaterBrook Press, 2001), 109.

11. "On Fairy-stories," in *The Tolkien Reader*, 55.

12. Lewis, *An Experiment in Criticism*, 141.

13. Walter Wangerin, *Swallowing the Golden Stone: Stories and Essays* (Minneapolis: Augsburg Books, 2001), 48.

14. O'Connor,*Mystery and Manners*, 96.

15. Coleridge, *Biographia Literaria*, 169.

16. Calvin Miller, "Ray Bradbury: Hope in a Doubtful Age," in *More Than Words*, 259.

17. Questions beginning with "I wonder . . ." are a hallmark of Jerome Berryman's "Godly Play" method, spinning off of Sofia Cavalletti's *Catechesis of the Good Shepherd*, which uses Montessori-style methods in teaching the Bible to young children. Sonja Stewart uses a similar approach in *Young Children and Worship*. See Appendix C: Suggested Resources.

18. Gregory Wolfe, *Intruding upon the Timeless: Meditations on Art, Faith, and Mystery* (Baltimore: Square Halo Books, 2003), 84.

CHAPTER 5: WHAT STORY ARE WE TELLING?

1. Kathleen Norris, *The Quotidian Mysteries: Laundry, Liturgy, and "Women's Work,"* 1998 Madeleva Lecture in Spirituality (New York: Paulist Press, 1998), 77.

2. I was first introduced to this concept by Richard Hays, professor of New Testament at Duke Divinity School. I'll come back to it later in this chapter.

3. "The Real Story," in *Touchstone Magazine: A Journal of Mere Christianity* (October 2005): 29.

4. *Intruding upon the Timeless*, 155.

5. Leland Ryken, "Thinking Christianly about Literature," in *The Christian Imagination*, 27-28.

6. From a live debate between Richard Hays of Duke Divinity School and Bart Ehrman of University of North Carolina, held at Duke in the spring of 2006: www.divinity.duke.edu/news/noteworthy/060428davincicode

7. See his memoir *Surprised by Joy: The Shape of My Early Life* (San Diego: Harcourt, 1955), chapter 11.

8. From the introduction to the radio drama of *The Man Born to Be King: A Play-Cycle on the Life of Our Lord and Saviour Jesus Christ* (San Francisco: Ignatius Press, 1990), 14-15.

9. Tony Jones, *Postmodern Youth Ministry: Exploring Cultural Shift, Cultivating Authentic Community, Creating Holistic Connections* (Grand Rapids, MI: Zondervan, 2001), 196.

10. A phrase used by Hans Frei and other postliberal scholars to describe the biblical narratives.

11. O'Connor, *Mystery and Manners*, 53–54.

12. Frei, *The Eclipse of Biblical Narrative*, 280.

13. I remember one of my undergraduate professors decrying this tendency, using the example of how some people approach Matthew 19:24 as a case in point. Apparently historicists like to explain Jesus' analogy of the camel and the rich person by saying there really was a gate in Jerusalem called "The Needle," through which camels had to kneel in order to pass. So the historicists, rather ingeniously, are able to explain to us what Jesus "really meant." My professor's commentary was along these lines: "Well, actually, what Jesus really meant when he said 'it is easier for a camel to go through the eye of a needle than for someone who is rich to enter the kingdom of God' is that 'it is easier for a camel to go through the eye of a needle than for someone who is rich to enter the kingdom of God.' Jesus said what he meant and he meant what he said." It was one of the first times I grasped that Christ spoke in metaphor and hyperbole on purpose in order to convey meaning. He embedded the meaning into the form itself, and for us to try to extract it borders on needless dentistry.

14. Wesley A. Kort, *Story, Text, and Scripture: Literary Interests in Biblical Narrative* (University Park, PA: Pennsylvania State University Press, 1988), x.

15. See Appendix B for my further musings on the implications of form in how we teach the Bible to youth.

16. Davis, *Imagination Shaped*, 251.

17. Lewis, *An Experiment in Criticism*, 93–94.

18. Frederick Buechner, *Telling the Truth: The Gospel as Tragedy, Comedy, and Fairy Tale* (San Francisco: HarperSanFrancisco, 1977), 81.

19. From the anthology *Exploring and Proclaiming the Apostles' Creed*, ed. Roger E. Van Harn (Grand Rapids, MI: William B. Eerdmans Publishing Company, 2004), 173.

PART 4: STORYTELLING

INTRODUCTION TO PART 4

Epigraph. Wangerin, *Swallowing the Golden Stone*, 106.

1. See the online Webcasts of Urbana 2000, specifically of December 30 (evening session), at:
www.urbana.org/u2000.worshipgatherings.cfm

CHAPTER 6: WORSHIP AS STORY

Epigraph. William H. Willimon, *Pastor: The Theology and Practice of Ordained Ministry* (Nashville: Abingdon Press, 2002), 93.

1. Dan Kimball, *The Emerging Church: Vintage Christianity for New Generations* (Grand Rapids, MI: Zondervan, 2003), 16.

2. Robert Webber, *Ancient-Future Faith: Rethinking Evangelicalism for a Postmodern World* (Grand Rapids, MI: Baker Books, 1999), 101.

3. Unfortunately I don't have the time or space to explore the all-important role of cultural context as a vital aspect of setting. This section will focus primarily on physical space. However, check my blog for further musings on how cultural context influences worship-as-story: http://godhungryimagination.blogspot.com

4. Webber, *Ancient-Future Faith*, 108.

5. Kimball, *The Emerging Church*, 134.

6. Jones, *Postmodern Youth Ministry*, 97; emphasis theirs.

7. Willimon, *Pastor*, 104.

8. Webber, *Ancient-Future Faith*, 99.

9. See *The United Methodist Book of Worship* (Nashville, TN: The United Methodist Publishing House, 1992), 15. I'm indebted to both Fred Edie of Duke Divinity School and Robert Webber of Northern Seminary for suggesting this general fourfold pattern for worship with youth. In particular, see Robert Webber's article "Youth Worship: What's Negotiable" in the September 2006 issue of *Worship Leader* magazine.

10. See Robert E. Webber's *The Younger Evangelicals: Facing the Challenges of the New World* (Grand Rapids, MI: Baker Books, 2002), as well as the article "The New Monastics: Alternative Christian Communities," by Jason Byassee, *The Christian Century* (October 18, 2005); http://www.christiancentury.org/article.lasso?id=1399.

11. Dean and Foster, *The Godbearing Life*, 9.

CHAPTER 7: THE ART OF IMMERSION

Epigraph. Dean and Foster, *The Godbearing Life*, 15.

1. *See* George A. Lindbeck, *The Nature of Doctrine: Religion and Theology in a Postliberal Age* (Louisville, KY: Westminster John Knox Press, 1984), chapter 1 and following.

2. Ibid., 132.

3. Dean and Foster, *The Godbearing Life*, 64.

4. For a narrative description of the ancient baptismal rite, *see* William H. Willimon's excellent classic, *Remember Who You Are: Baptism, A Model for Christian Life* (Nashville, TN: The Upper Room, 1980), or see chapter 4 of Daniel T. Benedict Jr., *Patterned by Grace: How Liturgy Shapes Us* (Nashville, TN: Upper Room Books, 2007).

5. http://www.divinity.duke.edu/programs/youth/

6. St. Peter's Anglican Church in Tallahassee, Florida: http://www.saint-peters.net/index.cfm/referer/content.home.

7. See Appendix C, Suggested Resources.

8. Smith and Denton, *Soul Searching*, 133.

9. "On Poets and Poetry," in *The Christian Imagination*, 381.

10. *Selected Literary Essays*, 263.

11. O'Connor, *Mystery and Manners*, 34.

12. See Smith and Denton, *Soul Searching*, 133.

13. Lindbeck, *The Nature of Doctrine*, 34.

PART 5: PRACTICAL CONCERNS

INTRODUCTION TO PART 5

Epigraph. L'Engle, *Walking on Water*, 140–41.

CHAPTER 8: THE YOUTH PASTOR AS BARD

Epigraph. From Jimmy Davis's online article "Valuing Storytelling over the Story," http://www.youthspecialties.com/articles/topics/story/storytelling_over_story.php.

1. See Smith and Denton, *Soul Searching*, page 120.

2. Jones, *Postmodern Youth Ministry*, 39; emphasis his.

3. Lewis, *An Experiment in Criticism*, 82–83.

4. Ibid., 19.

5. Jones, *Postmodern Youth Ministry*, 213.

6. Davis, "Valuing Storytelling over the Story."

7. See the *Concise Oxford English Dictionary*, 11th edition.

8. Richard B. Hays, *The Moral Vision of the New Testament: Community, Cross, New Creation; A Contemporary Introduction to New Testament Ethics* (San Francisco: HarperSanFrancisco, 1996), 94.

9. John Dominic Crossan, *The Dark Interval: Towards a Theology of Story* (Niles, IL: Argus Communications, 1975), 86.

10. For more on parable, see R. Grace Imathiu, *Words of Fire, Spirit of Grace* (Milwaukee: True North, 2003).

11. Sayers, *The Man Born to Be King*, 17.

12. Julia Cameron, *The Artist's Way: A Spiritual Path to Higher Creativity* (New York: Penguin Group, 1995).

13. Janice M. Elsheimer, *The Creative Call: An Artist's Response to the Way of the Spirit* (Colorado Springs, CO: WaterBrook Press, 2001).

CHAPTER 9: NOTES FROM THE FIELD

Epigraph. O'Connor, *Mystery and Manners*, 34.

1. T. S. Eliot, "Burnt Norton," part 2, from *Four Quartets*, in *The Complete Poems and Plays 1909–1950* (New York: Harcourt Brace Jovanovich, 1971), 119.

2. http://www.youthspecialties.com/free/programming/underground/simulation.php.

3. See information provided by Voice of the Martyrs, http://www.persecution.com/.

4. From *Polishing the Petoskey Stone: New and Selected Poems* (Wheaton, IL: Harold Shaw Publishers, 1990), 58.

5. *Dave and the Giant Pickle* is an animated video by VeggieTales (1996).

6. Some might object to Daniel being the main representative of the Exile. What about the other prophets? What about Nehemiah? My main thought is that Daniel makes the most sense because his story is one that children learn early on. It's hard to find a teachable narrative for the other prophets. So as youth workers, we start

with what our kids already know. Our goal is to weave together the disconnected parts before we teach them anything new.

7. I was delighted when the United Methodist Publishing House used a variation of these time-line exercises for their *Claim the Name* confirmation curriculum (see *Claim the Name: Confirmation Teaching Plans for 39 Weeks* [Nashville, TN: Cokesbury, 2001]). Another cool resource is *The Timechart History of the World* (Chippenham, England: Third Millennium Press, 2004). It's based on an original Victorian wall chart published in 1890 and opens up into a long, visually illustrated "tree" that concurrently depicts biblical history, dynasties of different people groups around the world, and major events. It's not the most politically correct piece of work, but it's fascinating.

8. Jenson, "How the World Lost Its Story."

9. O'Connor, *Mystery and Manners*, 192.

APPENDIX A: "IMAGINATIVE INTELLIGENCE"?

1. James W. Fowler, *Stages of Faith: The Psychology of Human Development* (New York: HarperCollins, 1995); Robert Coles, *The Moral Intelligence of Children* (New York: Random House, 1997); see also an interview with Robert Coles at http://www.pbs.org/newshour/gergen/february97/coles_2-21.html; John H. Westerhoff, *Will Our Children Have Faith?* (Harrisburg, PA: Morehouse Publishing, 2000).

2. Maria Harris, *Teaching and Religious Imagination: An Essay in the Theology of Teaching* (San Francisco: HarperSanFrancisco, 1991).

3. Howard Gardner, *Frames of Mind: The Theory of Multiple Intelligences* (New York: Basic Books, 1983).

4. For a quick summary, see www.en.wikipedia.org/wiki/Theory_of_multiple_intelligences

5. Barbara Bruce, *Seven Ways of Teaching the Bible to Children* (Nashville, TN: Abingdon Press, 1996).

APPENDIX B: FURTHER MUSINGS ON THE BIBLE AND NARRATIVE FORM

1. See http://www.dorothydunnett.co.uk/dunnettqa5.htm regarding the novel *King Hereafter* by British medievalist Dorothy Dunnett.

BIBLIOGRAPHY

Benedict, Daniel T. Jr. *Patterned by Grace: How Liturgy Shapes Us.* Nashville, TN: Upper Room Books, 2007.

Berryman, Jerome W. *Godly Play: An Imaginative Approach to Religious Education.* Minneapolis: Augsburg Books, 1994.

Brueggemann, Walter. *Texts under Negotiation: The Bible and Postmodern Imagination.* Minneapolis: Augsburg Fortress, Publishers, 2003.

Buckley, Ray. *Dancing with Words: Storytelling as Legacy, Culture, and Faith.* Nashville, TN: Discipleship Resources, 2003.

Buechner, Frederick. *The Alphabet of Grace.* San Francisco: HarperSanFranscisco, 1989.

_____. *Telling the Truth: The Gospel as Tragedy, Comedy, and Fairy Tale.* San Francisco: HarperSanFrancisco, 1977.

Coleridge, Samuel Taylor. *Biographia Literaria, or Biographical Sketches of My Literary Life and Opinions.* Edited by George Watson. London: J. M. Dent & Sons, 1975. First published in 1817.

Crossan, John Dominic. *The Dark Interval: Towards a Theology of Story.* Nile, IL: Argus Communications, 1975.

Davis, Ellen F. *Imagination Shaped: Old Testament Preaching in the Anglican Tradition*. Valley Forge, PA: Trinity Press International, 1995.

_____. *Wondrous Depth: Preaching the Old Testament*. Louisville, KY: Westminster John Knox Press, 2005.

Davis, Jimmy. "Valuing Storytelling over the Story." Youth Specialties online, 2004. www.youthspecialties.com/articles/topics/story/storytelling_over_story.php

Dean, Kenda Creasy and Ron Foster. *The Godbearing Life: The Art of Soul Tending for Youth Ministry*. Nashville, TN: Upper Room Books, 1998.

Frei, Hans W. *The Eclipse of Biblical Narrative: A Study in Eighteenth and Nineteenth Century Hermeneutics*. New Haven, CT: Yale University Press, 1974.

_____. *Theology and Narrative: Selected Essays*. Edited by George Hunsinger and William C. Placher. New York: Oxford University Press, 1993.

Green, Garrett. *Imagining God: Theology and the Religious Imagination*. San Francisco: Harper & Row, Publishers, 1989.

Hays, Richard B. *The Moral Vision of the New Testament: Community, Cross, New Creation; A Contemporary Introduction to New Testament Ethics*. San Francisco: HarperSanFrancisco, 1996.

Jenson, Robert. "How the World Lost Its Story." *First Things* 36 (October 1993):19-24. www.firstthings.com/ftissues/ft9310/articles/jenson.html.

Jones, Tony. *Postmodern Youth Ministry: Exploring Cultural Shift, Cultivating Authentic Community, Creating Holistic Connections*. Grand Rapids, MI: Zondervan, 2001.

Kimball, Dan. *The Emerging Church: Vintage Christianity for New Generations*. Grand Rapids, MI: Zondervan, 2003.

Kort, Wesley A. *Story, Text, and Scripture: Literary Interests in Biblical Narrative.* University Park, PA: The Pennsylvania State University Press, 1988.

L'Engle, Madeleine. *Madeleine L'Engle Herself: Reflections on a Writing Life.* Compiled by Carole F. Chase. Colorado Springs, CO: WaterBrook Press, 2001.

_____. *Walking on Water: Reflections on Faith and Art.* Colorado Springs, CO: WaterBrook Press, 2001.

Lewis, C. S. *An Experiment in Criticism.* Cambridge: Cambridge University Press, canto edition, 1992.

_____. *The Lion, the Witch and the Wardrobe.* New York: Macmillan Publishing Company, 1970.

_____. *On Stories and Other Essays on Literature.* San Diego, CA: Harcourt, 1982.

_____. *Selected Literary Essays.* Edited by Walter Hooper. Cambridge: Cambridge University Press, 1979.

_____. *The Silver Chair.* New York: Macmillan Publishing Company, 1953, 1970.

_____. *Surprised by Joy: The Shape of My Early Life.* San Diego, CA: Harcourt, 1955.

Lindbeck, George A. *The Nature of Doctrine: Religion and Theology in a Postliberal Age.* Louisville, KY: Westminster John Knox Press, 1984.

MacDonald, George. *The Heart of George MacDonald.* Edited by Rolland Hein. Vancouver, BC: Regent College Publishing, 2004. The essay "The Imagination: Its Functions and Its Culture" was first published in 1867.

_____. *Phantastes: A Faerie Romance,* with an introduction by C. S. Lewis. Grand Rapids, MI: William B. Eerdmans Publishing Company, 1981. First published in 1858.

Miller, Mark. *Experiential Storytelling: (Re)Discovering Narrative to Communicate God's Message*. Grand Rapids, MI: Zondervan, 2004.

Mills, David. "The Real Story." *Touchstone: A Journal of Mere Christianity* (October 2005):29.

Norris, Kathleen. *The Quotidian Mysteries: Laundry, Liturgy, and "Women's Work."* 1998 Madeleva Lecture in Spirituality. New York: Paulist Press, 1998.

O'Connor, Flannery. *Mystery and Manners: Occasional Prose*. Edited by Sally and Robert Fitzgerald. New York: Farrar, Straus & Giroux, 1970.

Rowling, J. K. *Harry Potter and the Sorcerer's Stone*. New York: Scholastic Press, 1998.

Ryken, Leland, editor. *The Christian Imagination: The Practice of Faith in Literature and Writing*, rev. edition. Colorado Springs, CO: WaterBrook Press, 2002.

Sayers, Dorothy L. *The Man Born to Be King: A Play-Cycle on the Life of Our Lord and Saviour Jesus Christ*. San Francisco: Ignatius Press, 1943.

_____. *The Mind of the Maker*. San Francisco: HarperSanFrancisco, 1987. Originally published in 1941 by Harcourt, Brace, New York.

Schakel, Peter J. *Imagination and the Arts in C. S. Lewis: Journeying to Narnia and Other Worlds*. Columbia: University of Missouri Press, 2002.

Shaw, Luci. *Polishing the Petoskey Stone: New and Selected Poems*. Wheaton, IL: Harold Shaw Publishers, 1990.

Smith, Christian with Melinda Lundquist Denton. *Soul Searching: The Religious and Spiritual Lives of American Teenagers*. New York: Oxford University Press, 2005.

Tolkien, J. R. R. *The Tolkien Reader*. New York: Ballantine Books, 1966.

_____. *The Letters of J. R. R. Tolkien*. Edited by Humphrey Carpenter. Boston: Houghton Mifflin Company, 2000.

Van Harn, Roger E., ed. *Exploring and Proclaiming the Apostles' Creed*. Grand Rapids, MI: William B. Eerdmans Publishing Company, 2004.

Wangerin, Walter, Jr. *Swallowing the Golden Stone: Stories and Essays*. Minneapolis: Augsburg Fortress, 2001.

Warren, Robert Penn. "Tell Me a Story." In *New and Selected Poems, 1923–1985*. New York: Random House, 1985.

Webber, Robert. *Ancient-Future Faith: Rethinking Evangelicalism for a Postmodern World*. Grand Rapids, MI: Baker Books, 1999.

West, Paul. *The Secret Lives of Words*. New York: Harcourt, 2000.

White, David F. *Practicing Discernment with Youth: A Transformative Youth Ministry Approach*. Cleveland, OH: Pilgrim Press, 2005.

Wiersbe, Warren W., comp. *Developing a Christian Imagination: An Interpretive Anthology*. Wheaton, IL: Victor Books, 1995.

Willimon, William H. *Pastor: The Theology and Practice of Ordained Ministry*. Nashville, TN: Abingdon Press, 2002.

_____. *Remember Who You Are: Baptism, a Model for Christian Life*. Nashville, TN: Upper Room, 1980.

Wolfe, Gregory. *Intruding upon the Timeless: Meditations on Art, Faith, and Mystery*. Baltimore: Square Halo Books, 2003.

Yancey, Philip, comp., and James Calvin Schaap, ed. *More Than Words: Contemporary Writers on the Works That Shaped Them*. Grand Rapids, MI: Baker Books, 2002.

ABOUT THE AUTHOR

Sarah Arthur is the best-selling author of *Walking with Frodo: A Devotional Journey through The Lord of the Rings* (Tyndale) and other youth resources. Before launching her freelance career, she served for seven years as the full-time youth director of Petoskey United Methodist Church in northern Michigan. She speaks around the country on issues related to story and spiritual formation, is a volunteer youth leader, and frequently writes youth resources for the United Methodist Publishing House. Her articles have appeared in *Relevant, Good News,* and *Devo'Zine.* Currently she resides in Durham, North Carolina, where she and her husband are graduate students at Duke Divinity School. For more information, visit her Web site: www.saraharthur.com. Also see her blog related to this book at http://godhungryimagination.blogspot.com.

OTHER TITLES OF INTEREST

Dancing with Words
Storytelling as Legacy, Culture, and Faith
by Ray Buckley

For people of faith, storytelling has special meaning. We are people of the Story, and we seek to identify and share our stories in nearly everything we do. *Dancing with Words* provides help for all church leaders—clergy and lay—to explore the history and importance of storytelling in faith development and to acquire basic storytelling skills.
ISBN 978-0-88177-407-8 • Paperback • 96 pages

Way to Live
Christian Practices for Teens
by Dorothy Bass and Don C. Richter

A collaborative effort of 18 teens and 18 adults, *Way to Live* explores Christian practices for youth. With a warm and encouraging tone, the contributors look at many different life practices as opportunities to infuse those practices with Christian meaning, as opposed to adding disciplines to our lives. They write about how to engage Christians in the real world with such varied topics as forgiveness, work, play, stuff, justice, music, prayer, food, and time. Get a free leader's guide at www.WaytoLive.org.
ISBN 978-0-8358-0975-7 • Paperback • 310 pages

The Godbearing Life
The Art of Soul Tending for Youth Ministry
by Kenda Creasy Dean and Ron Foster

Specifically designed to nurture the spiritual life of the youth leader, *The Godbearing Life* is a lively spiritual primer and practical guide for those who pastor young people. With soul-searing honesty, the authors rechart a course for youth ministry through classical spiritual disciplines of the church. The book identifies families, congregations, and mentoring relationships as the "holy ground" where young people are most likely to encounter God.
ISBN 978-0-8358-0858-3 • Paperback • 224 pages

**To order, call toll-free (800) 972-0433 or visit us at
www.UpperRoom.org/bookstore.**

Parables and Passion
Jesus' Stories for the Days of Lent
by John Indermark

Many writers who examine the parables of Jesus argue that they provide
a window into the acts of ministry carried out during Christ's journey to
Jerusalem. John Indermark takes us even deeper into that journey, holding
up the lessons of the parables Jesus told in light of his betrayal and death
on the cross. Considered in this way, the parables take on new significance,
becoming even more transparent and more clearly applicable in the lives
of Christians. Each week readers are provided with an overview, five daily
readings, and a "Sabbath" for reflection, review, or group study. [Editor's
note: This book is recommended as a personal or group formational experience for youth leaders, not for youth.]
ISBN 978-0-8358-1005-0 • Paperback • 176 pages

Creativity and Divine Surprise
Finding the Place of Your Resurrection
by Karla Kincannon

Just the book for youth leaders who need to feed their God-hungry imagination! *Creativity and Divine Surprise* helps readers discover their own
unique creativity as a means of deepening their spirituality. It couples
insightful meditations with thoughtful exercises to encourage spiritual
seekers who want to live a more creative and authentic life.
ISBN 978-0-8358-9812-6 • Paperback • 224 pages